PAINTING YOUR FLEA MARKET FINDS

Judy Diephouse and Lynne Deptula

NORTH LIGHT BOOKS
CINCINNATI, OHIO
www.artistsnetwork.com

Other fine North Light Books are available from your local bookstore, art supply store or direct from the publisher.

08 07 06 05 04   5 4 3 2 1

Library of Congress Cataloging-in-Publication Data

Diephouse, Judy
    Painting your flea market finds / Judy Diephouse and Lynne Deptula.-- 1st ed.
      p. cm.
    Includes index.
    ISBN 1-58180-482-2
    1. Furniture painting. 2. Decoration and ornament. 3. Used furniture. I. Deptula, Lynne
II. Title

    TT199.4.D54 2004
    745.7'23--dc22

                2003066228

Editors: Christina D. Read, Gina Rath
Production Coordinator: Kristen Heller
Designer: Joanna Detz
Layout Artist: Karla Baker
Photographers: Christine Polomsky and Tim Grondin

Metric Conversion Chart

TO CONVERT	TO	MULTIPLY BY
Inches	Centimeters	2.54
Centimeters	Inches	0.4
Feet	Centimeters	30.5
Centimeters	Feet	0.03
Yards	Meters	0.9
Meters	Yards	1.1
Sq. Inches	Sq. Centimeters	6.45
Sq. Centimeters	Sq. Inches	0.16
Sq. Feet	Sq. Meters	0.09
Sq. Meters	Sq. Feet	10.8
Sq. Yards	Sq. Meters	0.8
Sq. Meters	Sq. Yards	1.2
Pounds	Kilograms	0.45
Kilograms	Pounds	2.2
Ounces	Grams	28.3
Grams	Ounces	0.035

ACKNOWLEDGMENTS

We would like to say a special thank you to the terrific team of people at North Light Books. Kathy Kipp, Gina Rath, Chris Read, Christine Polomsky and Tim Grondin were a joy to work with. Their professionalism, expertise and support has made working on this book so much easier. Thank you again.

We would also like to thank the paint companies—Delta Ceramcoat and DecoArt Americana, and the brush company—Loew-Cornell, for supplying the paints and brushes needed to complete these projects. Your support in designing books and patterns is much appreciated.

ABOUT THE AUTHORS

Judy Diephouse and Lynne Deptula both reside in the Grand Rapids, Michigan area with their families. Having been business partners for more than 15 years, they truly love designing and teaching decorative painting. They feel that decorative painting is so relaxing, inspiring and just plain fun that it is a blessing to have such an enjoyable job! Judy and Lynne teach at decorative painting conventions and travel teach at seminars throughout the United States. Visit their website to view the more than 150 pattern packets and 15 books they have authored, pick up a few painting tips and download a "free pattern." Their website is: www.distinctivebrushstrokes.com.

Judy Diephouse
9796 Myers Lake Road NE
Rockford, MI 49341
Phone: 616-874-1656
Fax: 616-874-1713
E-Mail: DistinctJ@aol.com

Lynne Deptula
7245 Cascade Woods Drive SE
Grand Rapids, MI 49546
Phone: 616-940-1899
Fax: 616-940-6002
E-Mail: Dbrush1@aol.com

We dedicate this book
to our wonderful families and friends, who have given us constant support in so many ways. We would not have been able to accomplish all that we have without their encouragement and helping hands. A special thank you to Frank and Dave for being our foundations and best friends. We also want to thank the many, many painters we have met along the way in our travels who have become good friends.
Thanks for being there for us.

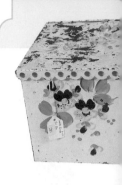

TABLE OF CONTENTS

CHAPTER ONE

The Thrill of The Hunt

THERE'S ALMOST NOTHING BETTER THAN AN OUTING AT THE LOCAL FLEA MARKET ON A BEAUTIFUL SUMMER'S DAY. TAKE A FRIEND OR TWO ALONG SO YOU CAN HELP EACH OTHER SPOT YOUR FAVORITE COLLECTIBLES, AND HAVE A GOOD LAUGH AT SOME OF THE OUTRAGEOUS ITEMS YOU'LL FIND.

THIS PARTICULAR FLEA MARKET IS IN HOWARD CITY, MICHIGAN, WHERE WE FOUND ALL THE PIECES WE PAINTED FOR THIS BOOK IN ONE ENJOYABLE AFTERNOON.

This display shows the availability of tinware, just waiting for your decorative touch. Notice the unique metal baby bathtubs from Europe—these could be turned into wonderful porch planters. Watering cans can be found at most flea markets—just do some comparative shopping to find the best price.

These days, reproductions are often so good they are hard to distinguish from the genuine antiques. If you are questioning whether a piece is a true antique, have it evaluated before you paint on it, as that can often diminish the value of the piece.

Take your time when browsing through the flea markets. Cluttered displays often produce unusual and charming finds at reasonable prices. It's a good idea to go with a painting friend, because two sets of eyes are better than one. And one person's ideas can spark more ideas from another person.

Another good hunting ground is old, hole-in-the-wall antique stores. We have found that the dirtier and more disorganized they are, the more likely they will yield unique treasures.

Did you notice, in the first photo, the fireplace screen lurking in the background? We did! Since painting on screens is becoming so popular, we thought this fireplace screen would look wonderful painted with a summery scene. There is great variety in the mesh size of fireplace screens, so choose a finer gauge screen for painting ease.

Don't be concerned about painting on a metal surface—there are an amazing number of paints and primers on the market that make it easy and quick to paint any metal surface.

I found it! I found it! I love it! Do you see what we saw? She's a ladybug, of course! This child's trike bike has a multitude of different surfaces: wood bars, metal handles, plastic seat and rubber wheels. To prepare it for painting, we used a red spray enamel primer, taping off any areas that we didn't want painted red. Then, we basecoated the rest of the areas in black or white. See page 124 for the cute and playful final results.

If you've never been to a flea market before, one of the first rules of thumb is "never pay the sticker price." Part of the fun is negotiating—the give-and-take between buyer and seller that often results in a great find for a very reasonable price. Here's a good example of "the wince"—a look on the buyer's face that says, "Oh, that price is still just a little too high; can you do a little better?" The good news is that the seller did give us a better price, and this old tin cannister became the pretty hand-painted vanity set you'll see on page 46.

The small, wooden sewing cabinet in the foreground of this photo will become the wonderful, shabby chic cabinet on page 28. As you can see, the author is negotiating a good price with the seller. Maybe this little cabinet is not in great condition, but a little wood filler and some sanding will fix it up.

Another valuable tip—bring husbands or sons to carry all your flea market goodies back to the car for you!

CHAPTER TWO

Materials Needed

Paints

We use Delta Ceramcoat and DecoArt Americana paints. These are nontoxic, water-based acrylic paints sold in bottles. Shake the bottles well before using to make sure the binder is mixed with the pigments. These paints can be thinned with water for a more transparent look or an ink-like consistency for stroke-work. Many different products on the market can be mixed with these paints to extend the drying time, or for easier flow. We personally do not use these products as we prefer using water, but please feel free to experiment.

Brushes

All of the brushes used in this book are from Loew-Cornell, Inc., 563 Chestnut Avenue, Teaneck, NJ 07666-2490, 1-201-836-7070. The series used include:

- no. 7000 rounds
- no. 7300 flat shaders
- no. 7550 flat wash brushes
- no. 7350 liners
- no. 7050 script liners
- JS liners no. 1
- no. 7850 deerfoot stippler
- no. 275 mops

Generally, acrylic brushes are made of synthetic fibers, such as Golden Taklon. Acrylic brushes hold up better when using acrylic paint. Natural hair brushes tend to swell when using water. The condition of your brushes determines the quality of your painting. It is very difficult for anyone to achieve nice strokework with a brush that has swelled or has loose hairs sticking out of it. There are several good brands of brushes on the market. Remember, you get what you pay for. To clean your brushes, we recommend DecoArt Americana's Brush Cleaner.

Water Basin

Many brands of water basins are available. A good basin will have ridges across one section of the bottom; pull your brush across the ridges to loosen and remove the paint on your brush. Grooves on the other side of the basin will hold your brushes in the water, which prevents the paint from drying in the brush. A high divider in the basin helps keep a supply of clean water on one side.

Stylus

A good stylus is useful for applying the pattern to the project, and for any fine dots and details you add to the painting. Often a stylus comes with points on both ends, one smaller than the other.

Palette Knife

A palette knife comes in handy when you need to mix paints.

Sponge

A small round sponge is used for background stippling, foliage or even to create clouds.

Tape

We recommend using quality transparent tape. Place the tape where you need it, then seal the edge with your finger to prevent paint from bleeding underneath the tape. You may also need masking tape and blue painter's tape.

Pencils

Always have a supply of sharpened no. 2 graphite and chalk pencils in your paint supplies. When tracing a pattern, one small area may have been omitted. Instead of trying to replace the pattern exactly, you can freehand the extra detail.

Toothbrush

An old toothbrush is the best tool for spattering and flyspecking. See page 17 for instructions.

Graphite Paper

Graphite paper is used to transfer the pattern onto the surface. It comes in sheets of gray, black and white at craft stores.

Palette

We use disposable waxed palettes. We do not use a wet palette, because we often blend colors on the brush before painting. If the palette is wet, the brush will pick up the moisture and it can be difficult to achieve a nice, gradual blend.

Stain

Minwax Ipswich Pine Wood Finish is a nice, medium-value warm brown stain/sealer. It antiques nicely, and provides a medium-value surface on which to paint.

Primer

Rust-Oleum makes excellent primers for tinware. We use Light Gray Automobile Primer on any tinware that could rust. You can use the Light Gray Automobile Primer, Gloss Protective Enamel in Flat White or any appropriate color (depending on the color of your project) to basecoat your tinware.

Tracing Paper

Tracing paper comes in a variety of sizes. It is readily available at art, hobby and office supply stores. See "Transferring the Pattern" (below) for instructions.

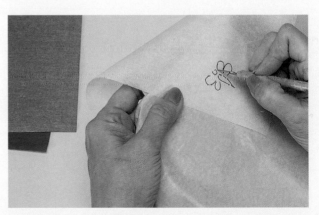

TRANSFERRING THE PATTERN If you have a dark background, use a light graphite paper. If the background is light, use a dark graphite paper. Place your traced pattern on your piece; tape one edge, if needed, to help secure it. Slide the graphite paper under the tracing, placing the graphite side down against the surface of the piece. Trace the pattern with a stylus.

CHAPTER THREE

Cleaning & Preparing Your Flea Market Finds

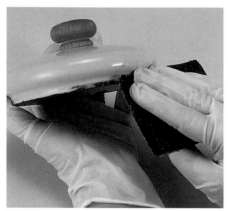

TINWARE Sand off rusty areas with heavy-duty sandpaper (60-grit). Wash the piece with warm soapy water. Dry completely.

TINWARE Spray the tinware with one layer of Rust-Oleum Light Gray Automobile Primer. Let cure for several days, depending on the humidity in your area. Check the surface by scraping over it with your fingernail; if cured you will not remove any primer. Basecoat as desired.

TINWARE On glossy tinware, such as this enamel coffee or camp pot, spray the entire exterior surface with Krylon Matte Finish spray. Let dry completely. This gives the surface some "tooth" for the paint to adhere to. Paint as desired.

METALWARE For metal surfaces, spray surfaces with Rust-Oleum Gloss Protective Enamel in Flat White or any other color, depending on your background color. Let cure for several days, depending on the humidity in your area. Basecoat as desired.

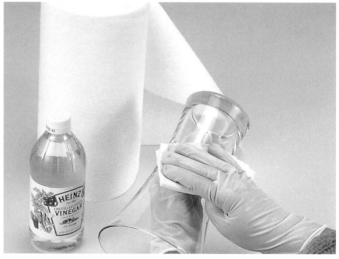

GLASSWARE Wash the glassware with warm, soapy water. Rinse well. Wipe the glass with a lint-free paper towel, moistened with white vinegar. Let dry completely.

STAINED, VARNISHED WOOD Use a medium, 150-grit sandpaper on a small hand sander to remove just the top layer of stain or varnish and to provide a good surface for the paint to adhere to.

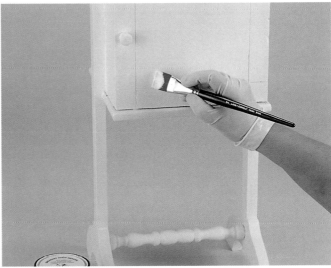

WOOD Sand to rough-up the old stained or varnished surface a bit. Apply primer to seal the surface, to stop stains from coming through your finished piece, and to give it a flat white finish.

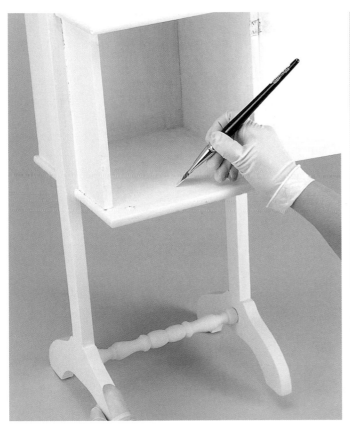

WOOD Prime all surfaces, inside and out. It will be necessary to apply two coats to cover darker surfaces. Let dry completely between coats of primer. Basecoat as desired.

PLASTIC Wash with soapy water. Let dry completely. Spray on a coat of gloss protective enamel that is close to the finish color, over the entire piece. Let dry. Apply basecoat colors to the piece.

CHAPTER FOUR

Painting
Techniques & Terms

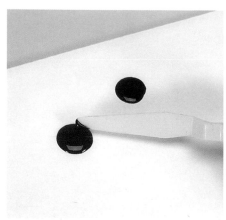

JUST A TOUCH On occasion, we may ask you to add just a touch of one color to another. This is usually done to tone the original color slightly. It should not make a huge change in the color, but will just tone it or brighten it as needed.

USING THE CHISEL EDGE Hold your brush perpendicular to the surface. Do not push on the brush, but allow the chisel edge of the brush to create a fine line.

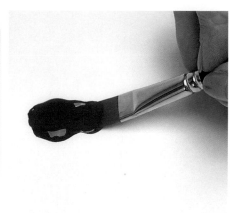

LOADING THE BRUSH To load the brush, dip the brush into the paint. Brush out onto the palette until the paint is halfway up the bristles. Turn the brush over and repeat to evenly load on both sides.

DOUBLE-LOADED BRUSH Dip one corner of the brush into one color and the other corner into the other color. Blend on the palette, until you get a gradual transition from one color to another.

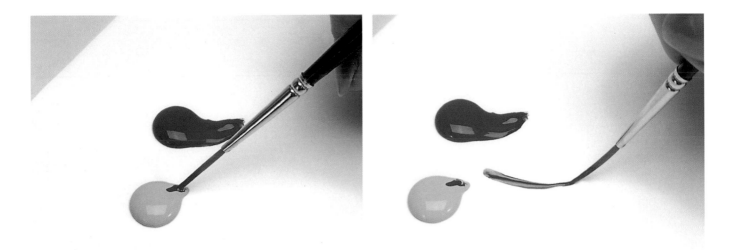

TIPPING A LINER Load the liner in the first color listed. Tip just the very tip of the brush into the second color listed. Do not blend on the palette. As you paint with the liner brush, the lighter color on the tip will start stronger and gradually fade out into the darker color as you paint the line. When you are asked to tip the brush, you are picking up a very small amount of the second color. If you dipped the brush, you would be picking up a larger amount of the second color.

SIDE-LOAD FLOAT Begin with a slightly damp brush. Slide one side of the brush next to the pile of paint; blend well on your palette. Remember to blend both sides of your brush to create a nice side-load float.

CORNER LOAD Just barely touch one corner of the brush into the paint.

CORNER-LOAD BLEND Blend the corner-loaded brush on the palette. You will use this blended brush when you need to tuck color into a small area.

LEAVES

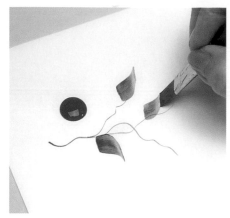  

ONE-STROKE LEAVES Load the brush with the color or colors listed. Hold the brush at an angle. Press the brush down the length of the bristles, lift up to the chisel edge of the brush and pull off slightly to the right or the left. If the brush is angled down to the right, you will pull off to the right. If it is angled to the left, you will pull off to the left.

SHADOW LEAVES Usually these are done with a smaller brush than usually used for the main leaves. Use very sheer color. Thin the paint with enough water so that you can still see the color, but the color is very transparent. Shadow leaves are done as a one-stroke leaf.

WIGGLE LEAVES Start with a double-loaded brush, that has been blended well on the palette. Begin one side of the leaf at the heaviest part of the leaf, pressing down and wiggling back and forth. Gradually lift the brush up as you go towards the tip of the leaf. The darkest color stays to the middle of the leaf. Do one side of the leaf, flip the brush over and repeat for the other side of the leaf.

FLOWERS

"C" STROKES Start with a side-loaded brush that has been blended well on the palette. Beginning with the brush on the chisel edge, press down to make the curve of the "C", and lift back to the chisel edge of the brush.

"S" STROKES Fully load the brush with paint. Start on the chisel edge of the brush, pulling to the left. Press the brush down as you pull to the right, and return to the chisel edge of the brush, as you pull again to the left.

STROKE FLOWERS This petal can be done with a double-loaded or a side-loaded brush. This stroke petal is similar to the "C" stroke. Start on the chisel edge of the brush to paint one side of the petal. When you press down for the curve of the "C", make a little wave for the top ruffle of the petal. Pull back up to the chisel edge of the brush to paint the other side of the petal.

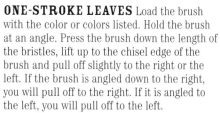

STROKE ROSES

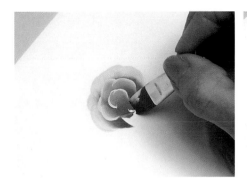

STROKE ROSES—BACK PETALS
With a double-loaded brush, make the back petal of the rose center. These petals are ruffly "C" strokes, each layer smaller than the one before.

CLOSING WITH FRONT PETALS Starting with the smallest center-back petal, reverse the curve of the "C" stroke, and have the top edges of these two strokes (back and front) make a circle. You should be making circles inside of circles. Paint the last front petal with pressure, to create the bowl of the rose.

SIDE PETALS Stand on the chisel edge of the brush, at the side of the rose bowl. Apply pressure and allow the brush to curve naturally, returning to the chisel edge as you pull the end of the petal into the bowl. Do not curve your brush as you do this petal, but allow the brush to curve as you are pulling up to the chisel edge.

SIDE PETALS, OTHER SIDE Repeat the stroke on the other side of the rose, but have the ends of the petals stagger so the tips do not touch.

LOWER PETALS Finish the rose with two smaller petal strokes, halfway under the larger side petals.

CALYX Using a liner, paint thin irregular lines on both sides of the bud for the calyx.

ROSEBUD Begin with a "C"-shaped stroke, with the curve pointing up. Next, start at the same place with the second "C" stroke, with the curve pointing down.

8 EASY PAINTING TECHNIQUES

FALL-AWAY BLOSSOMS Using a side-loaded or double-loaded brush, start the base of the fall-away blossoms with a group of three or four "C" strokes. As you trail off from the original flowers, make the "C" strokes smaller and lighter, until they fade away.

CHECKS Load your brush evenly. Stay on the chisel edge of the brush as you paint the checks. Do not have the corners touch. Then you will have room to adjust the size of the checks slightly as you match the end with the beginning checks. Always do two rows at one time. Begin your checks on the back of the piece, so if you need to adjust the size it is not so noticeable.

CIRCLE HIGHLIGHTS Use a side-loaded brush, with a little more moisture in the brush than usual. Tap in the color where the highlight is needed, using the clean side of the brush to soften the edges of the highlight area. Soften the edges completely around to form a circle.

BRUSH MIX Use the brush to pick up two or more colors, and create another small mound of paint. Use the brush to mix these colors together. Repeat this process often, so there will be slight variations in the mixed color. This effect creates more interest in the painting.

WET-INTO-WET Apply wet paint right on top of wet paint. This allows the colors to blend together.

FLYSPECKING Tap an old, damp toothbrush into the paint. The thinner the paint, the larger the flyspecking dots will be. (We recommend that you do not use your husband's toothbrush for this.)

FLYSPECKING Run your fingernail along the brush. This is definitely not good for a manicure! Maybe it's a good reason to go and have a manicure afterwards.

DOT FLOWERS These are simple flowers. They are made using your stylus or the wood end of a brush. Simply dip into fresh paint and dot on the surface.

STIPPLING Using a deerfoot brush to stipple, load the toe of the brush with paint. This is the longest end of the bristles. Start where the stippling should be the darkest and work toward the lightest edges. Pounce the brush up and down lightly in the area.

LEMONADE COOLER

Insulated aluminum cooler

HOW MANY OF YOU REMEMBER HAVING A METAL COOLER LIKE THIS? I FOUND THIS IN QUITE GOOD SHAPE AND STILL USABLE. BUT THE SILVER METAL COLOR ISN'T THAT ATTRACTIVE. SO LET'S MAKE IT THE CENTER ATTRACTION AT THE NEXT PICNIC.

MATERIALS

Loew-Cornell Brushes

☆ JS liner no. 1
☆ Series 7350 no. 6 liner
☆ Series 7300 nos. 6, 8, 10, 14, 16 and 20 flat shaders

Additional Supplies

☆ masking tape
☆ graphite paper
☆ tracing paper
☆ Rust-Oleum White Flat Protective Enamel
☆ spray acrylic varnish
☆ stylus

PAINT: DELTA CERAMCOAT ACRYLICS

Spice Brown	Colonial Blue	Black Cherry	Spice Brown + Black (3:1)
Dark Forest Green	Black	Pretty Pink	Sea Grass
Light Foliage Green	Caribbean Blue	Old Parchment	Forest Green
Bright Red	White	Denim Blue	Sea Grass + Forest Green (2:1)
Midnight Blue	Light Ivory	Midnight Blue + Black Cherry (1:1)	

PATTERNS

These patterns may
be hand-traced or
photocopied for
personal use only.
Enlarge at 200
percent to bring
up to full size.

LEAVES AND STRAWBERRIES

1 Clean the cooler with any of the new orange cleaning products, using a non-scratch scrubbing pad. Allow the cooler to dry thoroughly before basecoating. Tape off the opening of the cooler and the spout, so the paint can't get inside while spraying. Basecoat the cooler with Rust-Oleum White Flat Protective Enamel. This product will help to prevent any rusting on the cooler and is the basecoat color for the design. Allow the basecoat to dry and cure for a couple of days. Trace on the pattern, using the graphite paper. Trace on the least amount of pattern you are comfortable with.

2 Use a JS no. 1 liner and thinned Spice Brown to add the loose vining that comes from each side of the spout and meets at the back of the cooler. Do these vines loose and free. Do not overdo. You can always add more later.

 Tip

When painting on something that has ridges, like this cooler, you may need to thin your paint so it will flow into the ridges. Do not be concerned if there are places on the cooler not covered with paint. You will not notice this when you have completed the painting.

3 Using a no. 16 flat, double load the brush with Dark Forest Green and Light Foliage Green. Blend your brush well on the palette before painting the leaves, in order to achieve a gradual change in color from light to dark.

4 Using a no. 10 flat, basecoat the strawberries with Bright Red.

5 Use the same brush to pick up a corner load of Black Cherry. Blend on your palette. Shade the side of the strawberry closest to the bottom of the cooler.

6 Use a no. 14 flat, with a side-load float of Pretty Pink, to highlight the other side of the strawberries.

7 To make the strawberries look like they haven't completely ripened, float a tint of Old Parchment, using a no. 10 flat, along the top or along the bottom of the berry. This creates a little more interest to the berries.

8 Using a JS no. 1 liner and Black Cherry, randomly dot some seeds on the berries.

9 Highlight some of the seeds, on the highlighted area of the strawberry, with Old Parchment, using a no. 1 liner.

10 Double load a no. 6 liner with Dark Forest Green and Light Foliage Green. Add three to four small stroke leaves on the top of each berry.

11 Use a no. 8 flat to basecoat the blueberries with Denim Blue.

12 Use a no. 8 flat to shade the stem ends of the berries with a brush mix of Midnight Blue and Black Cherry (1:1). Brush mix these colors so there is some variation in the shading of the berries.

13 Use a no. 8 flat, with a side-load float of Colonial Blue, to highlight the other side of the berries.

14 Using a no. 1 liner with Black, add a small star-shaped blossom end on the highlighted side of the berry.

15 Use a no. 6 flat, with a side-load float of Caribbean Blue, to add an irregular "C" stroke around each star-shaped blossom end.

16 Using a no. 1 liner with White, add a fine highlight line on the upper part of the berry. You do not need to do this to every berry.

17 Basecoat the cherries with Bright Red, using a no. 10 flat.

18 Using the same brush, double load with Bright Red and Black Cherry. Blend on your palette. Shade the bottom side of the cherries.

19 Load the same brush with Bright Red. Touch one corner into White and blend well on your palette until that corner becomes a light pink. Highlight the other side of the cherry.

20 Highlight the cherry with a side-load float of White, using a no. 10 flat. Paint a large "C" stroke on the highlighted side of the cherry.

21 Corner load a no. 10 flat with Black Cherry. Add a small "C" stroke at the top of the cherry, where the stem would attach to the cherry.

22 Use a no. 1 liner, with a brush mix of Spice Brown and Black (3:1), to add stems to the cherries, which will connect them to the original vining. Add stems to any strawberry or blueberry that is not connected to the vining.

23 Using the same brown mix and brush, add stems to the large leaves. Continue into the leaf to create the center vein. Add some loose tendrils wherever you need to loosen up the design.

24 With a mixture of Sea Grass and Forest Green (2:1), use a no. 8 flat to add some smaller one-stroke leaves along the vining and tendrils. This will also help to loosen the design.

25 Load a no. 8 flat with Light Ivory and touch one corner into Sea Grass. Blend slightly on your palette. Stroke in the petals of the flowers. Not every flower will have four petals; some may be partially hidden by a berry.

26 Double load a no. 6 flat with Old Parchment and Black Cherry. Blend slightly on your palette. Touch in the centers of the flowers with a small stroke.

27 Using a no. 1 liner, add a highlight dot of White in the centers of the flowers.

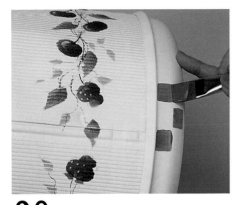

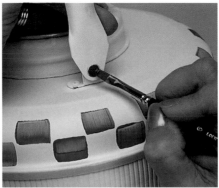

28 Using a no. 20 flat with Denim Blue, paint checks along the top and bottom of the cooler.

29 Dot some Bright Red on any rivets connecting the handle to the cooler. This adds another bit of interest and the finishing touch to your cooler.

Tip

- *Always start at the back of the piece. If you would need to adjust the size of the checks, it would not show up on the front.*

- *Never let the corners of the checks touch. This gives you room to negotiate the size of the checks, when you are returning to the original check. If each check touches and is perfectly shaped, you have no room for error.*

- *Stay up on the chisel edge of your brush while painting checks. This helps create a better shape to the checks.*

- *Do two rows at one time for an even look.*

30 Allow the painting to dry thoroughly. Erase any visible tracing lines. Varnish with three coats of your favorite acrylic varnish. Have fun serving your favorite summer beverage from this delightful cooler. Happy Summer!

SHABBY CHIC SEWING CABINET

ONE OF THE MOST POPULAR DECORATING TRENDS IS THE SHABBY CHIC LOOK. A BENEFIT OF THIS TREND IS THAT YOU CAN RECYCLE MANY OLD PIECES OF FURNITURE AND TURN THEM INTO TREASURES FOR TODAY'S DECOR. THIS PIECE COULD HAVE BEEN A SMOKING STAND OR SMALL SEWING STAND IN ITS FORMER LIFE. TODAY, IT COULD HOLD YOUR NEEDLE-WORK, SPECIAL KNITTING PROJECT, OR ANY OTHER HAND-WORK AND STILL LOOK GREAT IN A FAMILY ROOM, LIVING ROOM, OR EVEN BY THE SIDE OF A BED. THIS DESIGN COULD BE EASILY ADAPTED TO OTHER SMALL TABLES. HAVE FUN REDOING YOUR FOUND TREASURE.

Old wooden sewing cabinet

MATERIALS

Loew-Cornell Brushes

✶ Series 7300 nos. 2, 4, 6, 8 and 10 flat shaders
✶ Series 7550 1-inch (25mm) flat wash
✶ JS liner no. 1
✶ household brush

Additional Supplies

✶ electric hand sander
✶ fine-grit sandpaper
✶ Zinsser Primer Stain-Killer or Kilz Primer Stain Blocker ✶ painters tape
✶ round yellow artist's sponge ✶ graphite paper
✶ tracing paper ✶ stylus
✶ J. W. Right-Step Satin Varnish

PAINT: DELTA CERAMCOAT ACRYLICS

Forest Green	White	Moss Green	Sea Grass
Antique Rose	Glacier Blue	Cape Cod Blue	Violet Ice
Purple Dusk	Pale Yellow	Cape Code Blue + Glacier Blue (1:1)	Mello Yellow

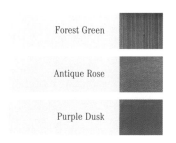

PATTERNS

Strokework pattern for step 18.

Strokework pattern for step 19.

These patterns may be hand-traced or photocopied for personal use only. Enlarge at 200 percent to bring up to full size.

STEMS, LEAVES & STROKE ROSES

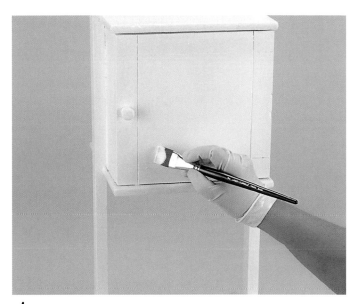

1 Sand the piece of furniture with an electric hand sander to smooth any rough areas and remove some of the old varnish. Prime the piece with a stain blocker like Zinsser or Kilz. Basecoat the piece with White. Allow it to dry thoroughly. Trace on the pattern, using your stylus and graphite paper.

2 Using a JS no. 1 liner with Forest Green, pull fine lines for the stems. Thin Moss Green with a little water and use a no. 16 flat to add some one-stroke leaves along the stems.

3 Double load the same brush with Forest Green and Sea Grass. Blend well on your palette so there is a gradation of color from dark to light. Add these leaves along the stems. Using a JS liner no. 1, pull a stem from the main stems into the center of these leaves with Forest Green.

4 Double load a no. 10 flat with Antique Rose and White. Put the White on the outside edges. If the White starts to turn pink, clean your brush and reload. (See technique for Stroke Roses on page 15.) Paint the stroke roses.

5 Add some rosebuds, using the same colors and the same brush.

6 Using the no. 1 liner and Forest Green, add calyxes to the rosebuds. Start at the base of the bud and pull a line up each side; then add a short line in the center of the bud.

7 Using the no. 1 liner, add stems to the lilies of the valley with Forest Green. Use a no. 4 flat to basecoat the lilies with Glacier Blue.

8 Using the no. 4 flat, shade the side of the lily closest to the center of the design, with a side-load float of Cape Cod Blue. Highlight the other side with a side-load float of White.

9 Apply a dot of White, using your stylus where the blossom attaches to the stem. Add a row of dots along the bottom edge of the lily.

10 Using the no. 1 liner, paint the stems of the lavender with Forest Green. Using the same brush and color, start a leaf right next to a stem. Apply pressure for the base of the leaf and pull out to a fine tip.

11 Double load a no. 2 flat with Violet Ice and Purple Dusk. The Purple Dusk will always go at the top edge of the blossoms. Touch one corner into one color and the other corner into the other color. Blend slightly on your palette. Paint fall-away blossoms for the lavender. (See technique on page 16.)

12 Add small filler flowers in any empty spaces. Double load a no. 4 flat with Pale Yellow and White. Keep the Pale Yellow to the outside of the petals. The flower is made with four "C" strokes. Using the same brush, touch in the centers of the flowers with a double load of Antique Rose and White.

13 Using a no. 2 flat, add some small, dark one-stroke leaves along the tendrils and stems with Forest Green.

14 Using a no. 8 flat, paint the ribbon with strokes of thinned Cape Cod Blue. Begin with two flat "C" strokes around the stems to form the wrapped ribbon around the flowers. Pull out the ties from each side. Apply pressure for the wider parts of the ribbon and raise up to the chisel edge of the brush for the thinner sections of the ribbon.

15 On the front door of the cabinet, use a small, round artist's sponge that has been dampened slightly to pounce lightly on the center area with Moss Green. Allow to dry.

16 Following the instructions for the stems, leaves and flowers on the top of the piece, paint the bouquet on the door.

17 Using a no. 8 flat with Purple Dusk, paint the checks in the four corners of the door.

18 Using a no. 6 flat with Antique Rose, paint the strokework along the top and bottom of the door. The design is a long "C" stroke with small one-strokes next to the "C" stroke. (See technique on page 14.)

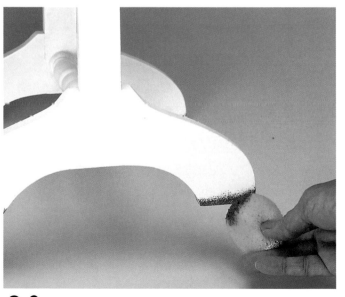

19 Using the no. 6 flat with Moss Green, paint the strokework design on each side of the door. The design is a series of two one-strokes going to the right, followed by two one-strokes going to the left. Repeat the design to fill in the designated space. Using a mix of Cape Cod Blue and Glacier Blue (1:1), paint the top of the door knob to add another touch of color.

20 Using the small, round sponge, lightly sponge the bottom of the legs with Forest Green.

FILLER FLOWERS & STRIPING

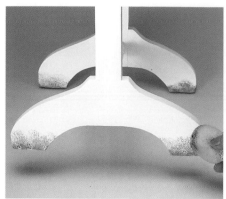

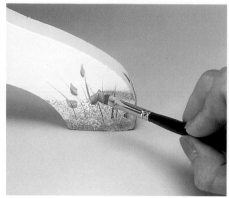

21 Using the same sponge, touch into Sea Grass and Moss Green and lighten the top of the Forest Green sponged areas. Keep these colors very soft at the top edge of the sponged area.

22 Using a no. 1 liner, pull some long grasses up the legs, using the same greens. Use a no. 8 flat, double loaded with Forest Green and Sea Grass, to add some one-stroke leaves along some of the grasses.

23 Using a no. 4 flat, add some yellow petal flowers in the grasses, similar to the filler flowers on the top. You may add dot flowers using your stylus or the wood end of your brush. Use any of the colors used to paint the flowers on the top of the piece.

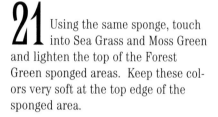

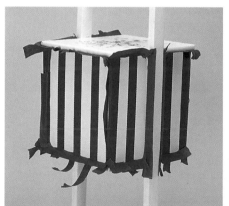

24 Tape off the sides and back of the cabinet to prepare to paint the stripes. Tape off the bottom and top edges of the cabinet to keep these areas clean while painting the stripes. Decide on the width of the stripes, keeping them in proportion to the size of your cabinet. Usually a one-inch taped stripe with a one-inch space works well. Taping off often takes twice as long as the painting of the stripes.

25 Using a 1-inch (25mm) flat and Mello Yellow, paint the stripes on the cabinet. Gently remove the tape while the paint is still wet so you can clean any bleeding under the tape.

26 Using the wood end of your brush, dot the rest of the legs with Antique Rose. Load the end and dot several times before reloading, which gives you a variation in the size of the dots.

27 If your piece has any turnings or spindles, paint these sections using a variety of the colors used for the flowers and leaves. Take your time and use a brush the width of the space you want to paint. Allow each area to dry before painting right next to it. Frame the top with corner lines of Purple Dusk, using a no. 1 liner. Use a fine-grit sandpaper and sand through some of the edges of the cabinet. How much you sand is a personal choice. You may like the older, shabby chic look with worn areas, or you may choose to keep your piece more pristine. It is your piece and it should please you. Allow the piece to dry thoroughly, erase any visible tracing lines and varnish with at least three coats of J. W. Right-Step Satin Varnish.

COMPLETED SEWING CABINET

PANSY TABLECLOTH

WE THINK OF PANSIES AS THE "SMILING FLOWERS" OF SUMMER. WHEN WE FOUND THIS COLORFUL TABLECLOTH, IT CALLED OUT FOR THE WONDERFUL COLORS OF PANSIES. THIS TABLECLOTH WOULD MAKE ANY LUNCHEON TABLE FEEL LIKE SUMMER! IT WOULD BE GREAT TO PAINT MATCHING PANSY NAPKINS . . . MAYBE WE'LL FIND THOSE ON OUR NEXT TREASURE HUNT!

Old stained tablecloth

MATERIALS

Loew-Cornell Brushes

✫ Series 7050 no. 1 script liner ✫ Series 7300 nos. 8, 10 and 14 flat shaders ✫ Series 7550 ¾-inch (19mm) flat wash

Additional Supplies

✫ Delta Textile Medium
✫ plastic palette knife
✫ waxed paper or plastic wrap

PAINT: DELTA CERAMCOAT ACRYLICS; DECOART AMERICANA (DA)

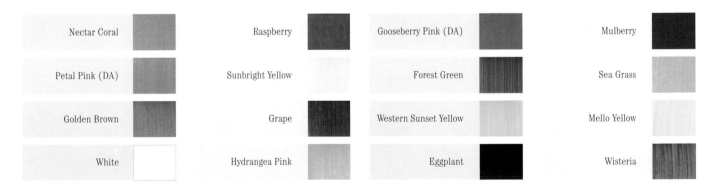

Nectar Coral	Raspberry	Gooseberry Pink (DA)	Mulberry
Petal Pink (DA)	Sunbright Yellow	Forest Green	Sea Grass
Golden Brown	Grape	Western Sunset Yellow	Mello Yellow
White	Hydrangea Pink	Eggplant	Wisteria

PATTERNS

yellow/peach pansy

peach/pink pansy

purple pansy

These patterns may be hand-traced or photocopied for personal use only. Enlarge at 154 percent to bring up to full size.

PEACH & PINK PANSY AND CORNER DETAIL

PAINT: DELTA CERAMCOAT ACRYLICS; DECOART AMERICANA (DA)

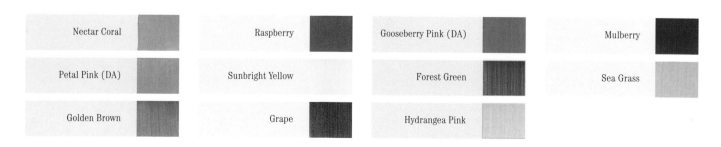

Nectar Coral	Raspberry	Gooseberry Pink (DA)	Mulberry
Petal Pink (DA)	Sunbright Yellow	Forest Green	Sea Grass
Golden Brown	Grape	Hydrangea Pink	

PEACH & PINK PANSY

1 Don't pass up that stained table-cloth—just paint over the stain to create a beautiful accessory for your home.

2 To paint on fabric, mix your acrylic paint colors with Textile Medium at a 2:1 ratio, using your plastic palette knife.

3 Place waxed paper or plastic wrap underneath the area of the fabric you are painting to protect paint from bleeding onto your painting table. Basecoat the three front petals of the pansy with Nectar Coral and Textile Medium on a no. 14 flat. Basecoat the two back petals of the pansy with Raspberry and Textile Medium.

4 Load a ³/4-inch (19mm) flat with Textile Medium. Dip one corner into Gooseberry Pink. Stroke back and forth on your pallette to blend well and make a side-load float. Shade the base of each pansy front petal with the prepared brush. Leave a sliver of the basecoat showing between each petal to maintain the shape of the flower. You do not need to dry the fabric between painting steps. Blending shade and highlight colors onto a damp surface works well and makes it easy to achieve soft shade and highlight areas.

5 Clean out your ³/4-inch (19mm) flat and reload with Textile Medium. Dip one corner into Mulberry to blend well and make a side-load float. Shade the base of each pansy back petal with the prepared brush.

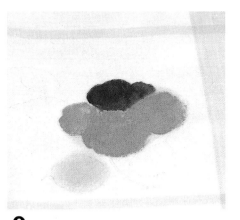

6 Use a no. 1 script liner to paint whisker strokes on the front three petals with Mulberry, thinned with Textile Medium.

7 Using a ³⁄4-inch (19mm) flat that is side loaded with Petal Pink thinned with Textile Medium, strongly highlight the outside edges of the back petals. Now, strongly highlight the front petals with a side-load float of Hydrangea Pink thinned with Textile Medium.

8 At the base of the main front petal, paint two yellow stamen comma strokes with Sunbright Yellow thinned with Textile Medium, using a no. 1 script liner.

9 Using a no. 10 flat loaded with Forest Green thinned with Textile Medium, basecoat the leaf shapes around the pansy blossom.

10 Double load a no. 10 flat with Forest Green and Sea Grass thinned with Textile Medium, and highlight the outside edges of each leaf with a wiggly or "nervous" stroke.

11 Use Forest Green thinned with Textile Medium on a no. 1 script liner to paint stems to the leaves, center vein lines in the leaves, and pull a few loose tendrils from the design. With the same brush, paint a ribbon tie winding around the stems with Raspberry thinned with Textile Medium. Then tint the leaves here and there with a side-load float of Sunbright Yellow on a no. 10 flat.

YELLOW & PEACH PANSY

PAINT: DELTA CERAMCOAT ACRYLICS

Western Sunset Yellow	Golden Brown	Mulberry	Mello Yellow
White	Nectar Coral	Hydrangea Pink	Sunbright Yellow
Forest Green	Sea Grass		

12 The Yellow and Peach Pansy is painted with the same techniques as the Peach and Pink Pansy. Remember to add Textile Medium to every color. The foreground petals are basecoated with Western Sunset Yellow and shaded with Golden Brown. The whisker lines are Mulberry. The petals are highlighted with a mix of Mello Yellow and a touch of White. The background petals are basecoated with Nectar Coral, shaded with Mulberry and highlighted with a mix of Nectar Coral plus Hydrangea Pink (1:1). The stamens are painted as small comma strokes of Sunbright Yellow. The leaves are basecoated with Forest Green and highlighted with a double-loaded brush of Forest Green and Sea Grass. The stems, vein lines and tendrils are Forest Green. The ribbon tie is painted with Nectar Coral.

PURPLE PANSY

PAINT: DELTA CERAMCOAT ACRYLICS; DECOART AMERICANA (DA)

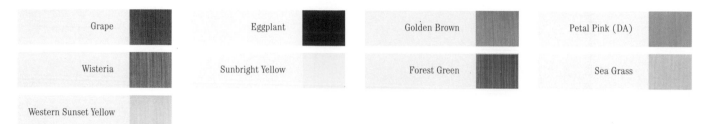

Grape	Eggplant	Golden Brown	Petal Pink (DA)
Wisteria	Sunbright Yellow	Forest Green	Sea Grass
Western Sunset Yellow			

13 The Purple Pansy is painted with the same techniques as the Peach and Pink Pansy. Remember to add Textile Medium to every color. All petals are basecoated with Grape and shaded with Eggplant. The whisker lines on the front three petals are painted with Golden Brown plus a touch of Western Sunset Yellow. Highlight the front petals with Petal Pink and the back petals with Wisteria. The stamens are painted as small comma strokes of Sunbright Yellow. The leaves are basecoated in Forest Green. Highlight with a double-loaded brush of Forest Green and Sea Grass. The stems, vein lines and tendrils are Forest Green. The ribbon tie is painted with Grape.

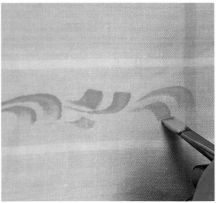

CORNER DETAIL

14 Remember to mix your paint with the Textile Medium to make painting smooth and easy and to help the paint adhere to the fabric. Use a no. 1 script liner for the fine lines and stay on the tip of the brush to achieve thin lines. I painted a plaid design with Raspberry, a few diagonal lines of Golden Brown, dots of Forest Green, a checkerboard of Gooseberry Pink (using a no. 8 flat) and spirals of Grape.

STROKEWORK BORDER

15 On your palette, make a 1:1 mix of Textile Medium and Sea Grass. Using a no. 8 flat, paint a simple border of comma strokes around all sides of the tablecloth to finish it off.

16 Paint the pansies in scattered squares on the tablecloth to create a light, casual design. This will become a favorite accessory in your home.

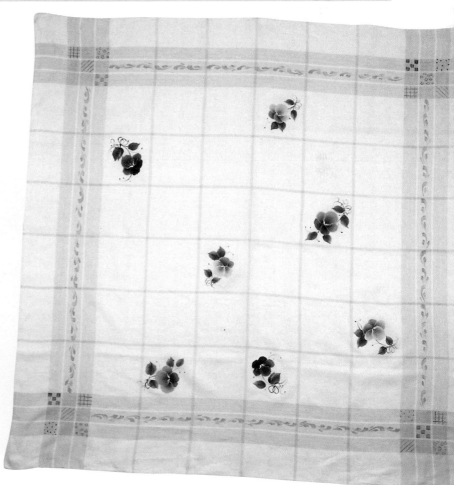

VANITY SET

WHAT A PRETTY WAY TO "ACCESSORIZE YOUR CLUTTER." THIS PAINTED TINWARE BOX WILL HOLD THAT EXTRA ROLL OF TISSUE OR MAKE-UP SUPPLIES. THE MINI-SHELF WILL LOOK ADORABLE FILLED WITH YOUR FAVORITE LOTIONS OR PERFUME BOTTLES!

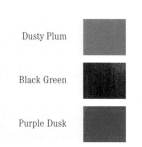

Rusted Tinware

MATERIALS

Loew-Cornell Brushes

✳ Series 275 1-inch (25mm) oval mop ✳ Series 7050 no. 1 script liner ✳ Series 7300 nos. 2, 4, 8 and 12 flat shaders ✳ Series 7550 nos. ³⁄4-inch (19mm) and 1-inch (25mm) flat wash ✳ JS liner no. 1

Additional Supplies

✳ gray graphite paper
✳ tracing paper
✳ J. W. Right-Step Satin Varnish ✳ Krylon Acrylic Crystal Clear Protective Clear Coating
✳ Rust-Oleum Light Gray Auto Primer ✳ stylus
✳ white chalk pencil

PAINT: DELTA CERAMCOAT ACRYLICS

Stonewedge Green	Butter Cream	Dusty Plum	Wisteria
Dark Forest Green	Royal Plum	Black Green	Pale Lilac
Butter Yellow	Spice Brown	Purple Dusk	Violet Ice
Pale Yellow			

PATTERNS

These patterns may be hand-traced or photocopied for personal use only. Enlarge at 118 percent to bring up to full size.

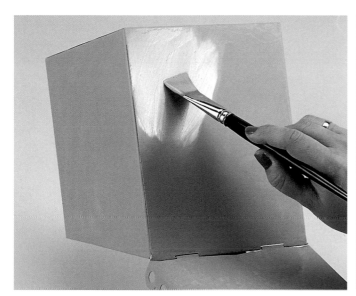

1 Sand off any rust and prime the metal surfaces with Rust-Oleum Light Gray Auto Primer. Let dry. Basecoat the outside and inside of the tinware box, but not the top of the lid, with Stonewedge Green on a 1-inch (25mm) flat. Apply two coats to achieve opaque coverage. Let dry completely between layers of basecoat.

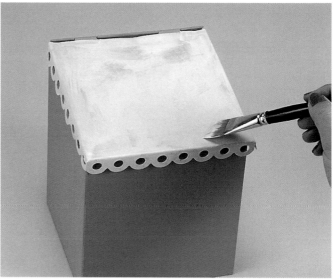

2 Using the same brush, basecoat the lid of the tinware box with Butter Cream. Apply two coats to achieve opaque coverage. Let dry completely between layers of basecoat.

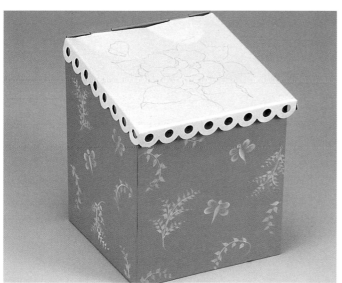

3 Using a liner brush and a no. 4 or no. 8 flat for the various sized leaves, paint the fern and dragonfly designs with slightly thinned Butter Cream. Using slightly worn gray graphite paper and a stylus, lightly transfer the rose pattern onto the lid of the tinware box.

4 Using a no. 12 flat and thinned paint, basecoat a sheer layer of Stonewedge Green on the leaves and Dusty Plum on the flower petals. The paint should be sheer enough so that you can still see your pattern lines when the paint dries.

5 Using a ³⁄4-inch (19mm) flat, side loaded into Dark Forest Green, softly float shading at the base of each leaf. Shade one half of each leaf. Then slide on the chisel edge of your brush and up the vein line. Shade the other half of each leaf, leaving a small line of your basecoat color showing to form a center vein line. For the rose petals, use the same brush, side loaded into Wisteria. Softly float shading at the base of each petal. Leave a sliver of the basecoat color showing between each flower petal; this will help to maintain the shape of your rose.

6 Deepen and widen the shading on the leaves, using the same brush side loaded again into Dark Forest Green. Using a no. 12 flat, side loaded into Dark Forest Green, shade behind the flips in the leaves to make them "pop out."

7 Deepen and widen the shading on the rose petals with a ³⁄4-inch (19mm) flat, side loaded again into Wisteria. Keep in mind that as you shade the base of each petal, you are also painting the outside edge of the petal next to the shaded area. Maintain the shape of the rose. Using a no. 12 flat, side loaded into Wisteria, shade behind the flips in the rose petals.

8 Deepen the "V" areas of the rose petals, with an additional side-load float of Royal Plum, on a ³⁄4-inch (19mm) flat. Royal Plum is a very strong color, so use it sparingly. This layer of shading should be contained within the first layers of Wisteria shading.

9 This is a fun step! Using a ³⁄4-inch (19mm) flat, side loaded sparingly into Black Green, separate overlapping leaves and tuck leaves behind the rose petal edges with soft side-load floats. This step will make the leaves fall behind the rose, and make the rose "pop out" on the tinware box lid.

10 Heavily sideload Pale Lilac on a no. 12 flat and highlight the outside edge of all rose petals. Blend over the highlight area to soften the color into the surface. If you should accidentally walk the highlight color back too far, it will cloud over the shade area. However, we can clear that up in the next step.

11 Use a ¾-inch (19mm) flat, side loaded into Royal Plum, to reinforce the shading of the rose petals that became cloudy during the highlight step. Deepen the throat of the rose with an additional shade of Royal Plum, until the proper depth is achieved.

12 Tint the outside edges of some leaves with a soft side-load float of Butter Yellow on a ¾-inch (19mm) flat. Notice how this really makes the leaves come to life with a soft glow.

13 Further tint the edges of some leaves with a soft side-load float of Wisteria. Use this color sparingly; it's so easy to overdo, because it looks so pretty. Just tint a few leaves.

14 With thinned Spice Brown on a no.1 script liner, paint the stems to the rose and the rosebud. Pull several areas of loose vining from behind the rose, and paint subtle vein lines on the rose leaves. Using the same brush, add a calyx to the rosebud by painting "nervous one-strokes" of Dark Forest Green at the base of the rosebud.

15 Heavily double load a no. 4 flat into Purple Dusk and Violet Ice to paint the small filler flowers. Keeping the darker color to the outside edge of each petal, paint very small "C" strokes to form the flower petals. Using the tip of a no. 1 liner brush and Pale Yellow, paint very small dots in the center of the full flower shapes. Paint the stamen lines of the main rose with very thin lines of Pale Yellow. Dot the outside curve of the stamen lines with tiny dots of Pale Yellow.

16 Paint the stem lines for the fern fronds with a no. 1 liner and thinned Dark Forest Green. Using a no. 4 flat and a sheer double load of Stonewedge Green and Dusty Plum, paint small fern leaves along the stemlines. Notice how the leaves become smaller as they approach the gracefully curved tip of the frond.

17 With thinned Purple Dusk and a no.1 liner brush, paint a line-work bow around the floral stems. Highlight the outside curves of the bow and the knot with thin top lines of Violet Ice.

18 Trim out the lid of the tinware box with line work of Wisteria. Use a no. 1 liner brush to paint a curved line around the lower half of each scallop, and paint three dashes between each curved line.

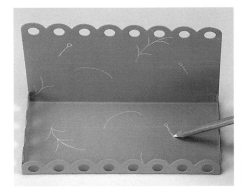

19 Using a white chalk pencil, indicate the placement of the ferns and dragonflies on your mini-shelf.

20 Load a no. 1 script liner with thinned Butter Cream, and paint in the stem lines of the ferns. With a no. 4 flat and thinned Butter Cream, paint the larger fern frond leaves with small one-stroke leaves. Notice how the leaves become smaller as they approach the gracefully curved tip of the fern frond.

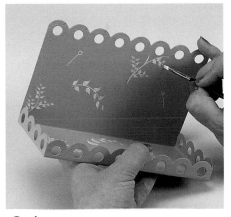

21 To paint the smaller one-stroke fern frond leaves, use a no. 2 flat and thinned Butter Cream.

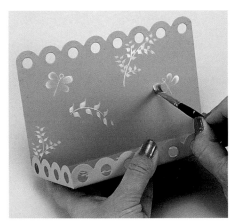

22 Paint the dragonfly wings as curvy "C" strokes, using a no. 8 flat side loaded into Butter Cream. Keep the color strongest around the outside edge of the wing. Let the color become slightly sheer as you come closer to the body. This will give the wings a translucent quality.

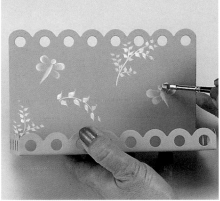

23 Paint the dragonfly bodies with a no. 4 flat, sideloaded into Butter Cream. Let the entire body and head receive some color. Keep more color on one side of the brush, to automatically shade as you basecoat.

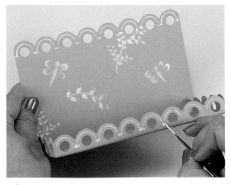

24 Load a no. 1 script liner with thinned Butter Cream. Paint curved lines, following the trim edge of the mini-shelf. Detail between each curved line with three dashes of the same color. Erase all visible pattern lines. Brush on one layer of J. W. Right-Step Satin Varnish, using a 1-inch (25mm) mop brush. Carefully varnish all the rolled edges and corners of the tin-ware. Let it cure for twenty-four hours. Then apply one coat of Krylon Acrylic Crystal Clear Protective Clear Coating.

AUTUMN TOTE

THIS WAS A HANDMADE TOTE FOR PICKING BERRIES. WHEN WE BOUGHT IT, IT HAD FOUR BASKETS INSIDE TO HOLD QUARTS OF BERRIES. IT WOULD HAVE BEEN EASY TO PAINT IT WITH A BERRY DESIGN, BUT WE WANTED TO GIVE IT A DIFFERENT THEME. IT WAS VERY ROUGH, SO IT NEEDED TO BE SANDED WELL. ONCE THAT WAS COMPLETED, WE DECIDED IT WOULD LOOK GREAT FOR THE FALL, FILLED WITH LEAVES, COLORED GOURDS AND BITTERSWEET. IF YOU CAN'T FIND AN OLD TOTE LIKE THIS, MAYBE YOU CAN GET YOUR FAVORITE WOODCUTTER TO MAKE YOUR OWN AUTUMN TOTE.

MATERIALS

Loew-Cornell Brushes

✶ Series 7300 nos. 2, 4, 6, 8, 10, 12, 16 and 20 flat shaders ✶ Series 7350 no. 6 liner ✶ Series 7550 ³⁄₄-inch (19mm) and 1-inch (25mm) flat wash ✶ JS no. 1 liner

Additional Supplies

✶ tracing paper
✶ graphite paper
✶ old toothbrush
✶ J. W. Right-Step Satin Varnish ✶ turpentine
✶ rubber gloves
✶ soft cloth ✶ cotton swabs ✶ Burnt Umber oil paint ✶ stylus

PAINT: DELTA CERAMCOAT ACRYLICS

Flesh Tan		Toffee		Burnt Umber		Antique Gold	
Butter Yellow		White		Mocha Brown		Dark Forest Green	
Timberline Green		Light Timberline Green		Georgia Clay		Straw	
Moroccan Red		Black Cherry		Bright Red		Pine Green	
Pine Green + Dark Forest Green (1:1)		Bittersweet Orange		Sea Grass		Calypso Orange	
Black Green		Brown Iron Oxide		Tangerine		Gamal Green	
Dark Burnt Umber		Timberline Green + Dark Forest Green + Mocha Brown (1:1:1)		Butter Yellow + White (1:1)		Tangerine + Bittersweet Orange (1:1)	

PATTERNS

PATTERN FOR THE HANDLE

Pattern is shown here full size.

This pattern may be hand-traced or photocopied for personal use only. Enlarge at 167 percent to bring up to full size.

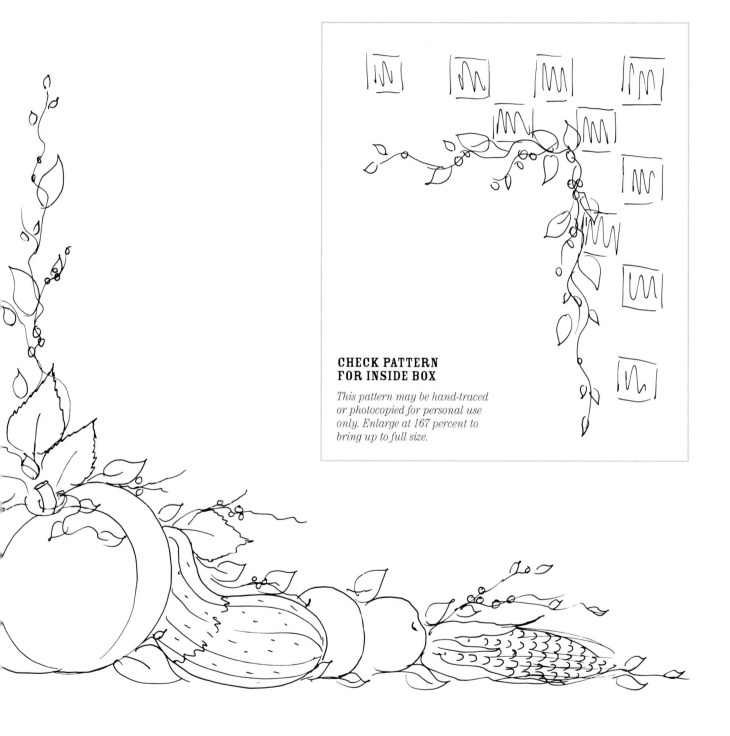

**CHECK PATTERN
FOR INSIDE BOX**

*This pattern may be hand-traced
or photocopied for personal use
only. Enlarge at 167 percent to
bring up to full size.*

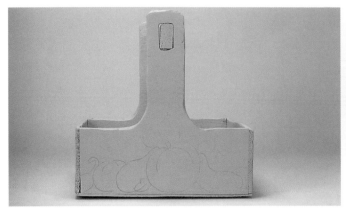

1 Basecoat the entire box with Flesh Tan. Allow to dry thoroughly. Trace on the pattern.

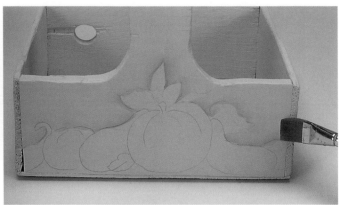

2 Using a 1-inch (25mm) flat, with a side-load float of Toffee, shade behind all of the objects. Keep this shading very soft, creating a soft shadow behind the design.

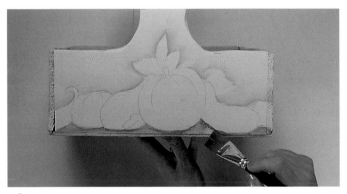

3 Use the same brush, with a side-load float of Burnt Umber. Float below the design to create the ground under the objects.

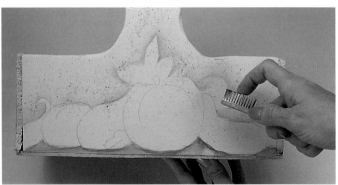

4 Using an old toothbrush, flyspeck with Burnt Umber around the design, on the handles and inside the tote.

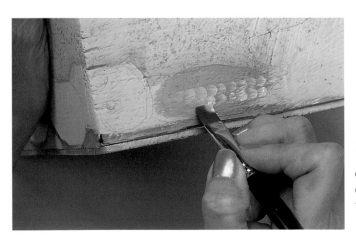

5 Basecoat the corn with Antique Gold, using a no. 12 flat. Use the same brush to side-load float a brush mix (see page 16) of Butter Yellow and White, to make "C" strokes down the center of the corn, starting at the tip. Then do the same above and below the center row.

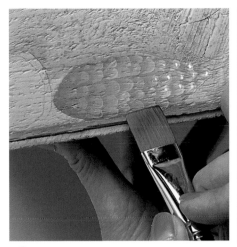  

6 Using a no. 1 liner, add White highlights on some of the top and center kernels of corn. Shade both the sides and end of the corn with Mocha Brown, using a no. 20 flat. Make the shading heaviest at the end and soften the sides as you go to the tip of the ear.

7 Use a no. 8 flat, double loaded with Timberline Green and Light Timberline Green, to pull three long strokes for the husks. Start on the flat of your brush and pull up to the chisel as you complete the stroke.

8 Use the same brush with a side-load float of Dark Forest Green, to shade between the leaves, along the back, and on the lower edge of each leaf.

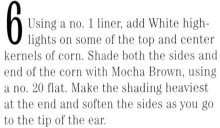
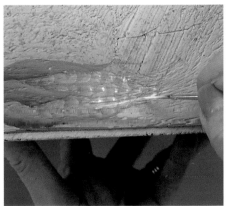 

9 Using a no. 20 flat, with a side-load float of Georgia Clay, shade the corn next to the leaves. Using a no. 1 liner, add fine lines of corn silk with Mocha Brown, Antique Gold, Butter Yellow and White. Start with the darkest color and work up to the lightest.

10 Basecoat the apples with Straw, using a no. 12 flat. The smaller apple in the background is shaded with Moroccan Red. Wet the apple with clean water, side load a ¾-inch (19mm) flat with Moroccan Red and shade one section of the apple. It takes several soft floats to achieve the shading you desire.

11 The shading along the top of the apple is lighter than the shading along the bottom. Allow some of the Straw to show for the highlighted area.

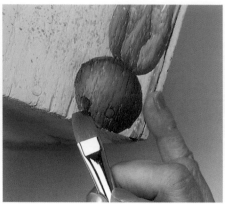

12 Shade the lower side of the apple with a side-load float of Black Cherry, using the no. 20 flat. Use a no. 12 flat with a side-load float of Black Cherry to make a "C" stroke for the stem hollow.

13 The larger front apple is first shaded with Bright Red. Follow the same steps as for the other apple. Deepen the shading with Black Cherry.

14 Basecoat the summer squash with Straw, using a no. 12 flat. The basecoating on the squashes and pumpkins may take two coats. Allow the paint to dry between coats. Make the bumps on the skin of the squash with a side-load float of "C" strokes using Antique Gold. Using a no. 20 flat, with a side-load float of Mocha Brown, shade along the lower side of the squash. Add a touch of shading on the curve on the top side.

15 Highlight the summer squash with Butter Yellow. Corner load a no. 20 flat, touch in the area of the highlight and soften the edges of the area to create a circle highlight. Repeat the highlight with White, making sure the edges of the highlighted area fade out softly.

16 Use a no. 12 flat to basecoat the bottoms of the gourds with a mix of Pine Green and Dark Forest Green (1:1). Basecoat the top section with Bittersweet Orange. Leave the area where the colors meet a little jagged.

17 Use a no. 6 liner to tap into thinned Sea Grass and then into Light Timberline Green, then pull the stripes on the gourd up from the bottom. Touch the brush into Calypso Orange and/or Straw and continue the stripes into the yellow section. Add touches of the same color between the stripes.

18 Use the same highlighting method, as done on the summer squash in step 15, to highlight the orange section with Calypso Orange and the green section with Sea Grass, using a no. 20 flat. Repeat these highlights with the same colors, adding a touch of White to each color. Shade the gourd in the area behind the pumpkin with a float of Georgia Clay.

19 Shade the lower side of the gourd with a side-load float of Black Green, using a no. 20 flat.

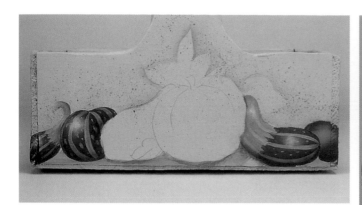

20 Basecoat the gourd with Pine Green, using a no. 12 flat. Use a no. 6 liner, with thinned Light Timberline Green and Sea Grass, to make the stripes and touches of color between the stripes. Add a highlight with Sea Grass, using a no. 12 flat. Repeat the highlight with a touch of White added to the Sea Grass. Shade the bottom and side of the gourd next to the Hubbard squash with a side-load float of Black Green, using a no. 20 flat.

21 Stroke in the stem using a no. 4 flat double loaded with Toffee and Burnt Umber.

22 Use a no. 20 flat to basecoat the Hubbard squash with Butter Yellow. For the bumps on the squash, use a no. 12 flat with a side-load float of Antique Gold to make "C" strokes. Shade the squash along the bottom and behind the pumpkin with a side-load float of Mocha Brown, using a no. 20 flat.

23 Use a no. 20 flat, with a side-load float of Butter Yellow, to highlight the top edge of the squash. Using the same method as for the summer squash in step 15, make a center highlight with a mix of Butter Yellow and White (1:1). Repeat the highlight with White.

24 Basecoat the pumpkin with Georgia Clay, using a no. 20 flat. Use the same brush to touch one side into Brown Iron Oxide; blend well on your palette. Shade the bottom of the pumpkin and next to both sides of the center section.

25 Use a no. 20 flat to highlight the pumpkin edges and sides and center-section sides with a side-load float of Tangerine. Create the circle highlight on the center and right sections with a side-load mix of Tangerine and Bittersweet Orange (1:1). Repeat the highlight with just Bittersweet Orange.

26 Using a no. 6 flat, basecoat the stem with Burnt Umber; it may take two coats. Use the same brush and tap into White, then overstroke the stem with the dirty White.

27 Load one side of a no. 16 flat with Gamal Green. Touch the other side randomly into Antique Gold, Timberline Green and Mocha Brown. Paint the largest leaves using the wiggle technique. (See page 14).

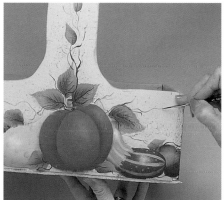

28 Using the same brush with the same colors, add the one-stroke leaves around the design. Using a no. 1 liner with Dark Burnt Umber, add some tendrils and stems to these leaves.

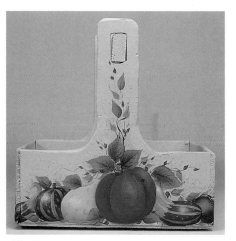

29 Use a no. 10 flat, with a brush mix of Timberline Green, Dark Forest Green, and Mocha Brown (1:1:1), to make a dried-out leaf color. Thin the paint with water and add some sheer leaves along the vining. Use a no. 6 flat with a brush mix (see page 16) of Dark Forest Green and Gamal Green to add some small, dark one-stroke leaves.

30 Using a no. 2 flat, basecoat the berries with Tangerine. Shade the stem end of the larger berries with a side-load float of Black Cherry. Highlight the larger berries with a side-load float of Bittersweet Orange. Use a stylus or the tip of the no. 1 liner to add a dot of Calypso Orange to each berry.

31 Paint checks in the corners on the inside of the tote using a ³/4-inch (19mm) flat and Gamal Green. As you work your way away from the corner, make the checks lighter and lighter, until they fade out.

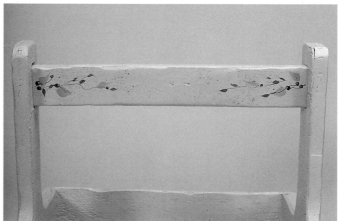

33 Add some of the same detail on the handle.

32 Following the previous instructions in steps 28 – 30, add some tendrils, sheer leaves, small dark leaves and bittersweet berries in each corner.

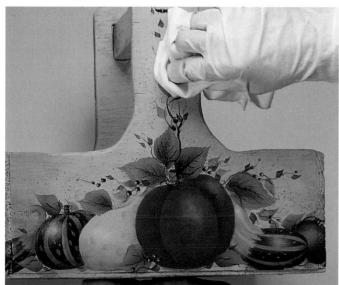

34 Varnish the tote completely with one coat of J. W. Right-Step Satin Varnish. Wear rubber gloves and use a soft cloth that has been moistened with turpentine to apply some Burnt Umber oil paint over the entire piece. Then use a clean, soft cloth and cotton swabs to wipe out the center highlight area on each vegetable. Use the Burnt Umber, where needed, to deepen the shade areas. The depth of antiquing is a personal choice. Soften all of the edges between the clean-out areas and the shade areas. There should not be any hard lines of antiquing.

35 Allow the antiquing to dry several days before applying two more coats of satin varnish. Fill the tote with Fall leaves, gourds, squashes, small pumpkins and bittersweet. What a wonderful Fall centerpiece for your counter or table.

AMERICANA CAMP POT

Enamel Camp Pot

THIS ANTIQUE ENAMEL CAMP POT IS GOING TO BE FILLED WITH RED GERANIUMS AND PLACED ON THE PORCH TO CELEBRATE SUMMER. THIS DESIGN WOULD LOOK EQUALLY FINE ON AN OLD BUCKET OR A RUSTIC WINDOW BOX . . . JUST KEEP LOOKING AROUND AT THE FLEA MARKETS FOR YOUR PERFECT SURFACE.

MATERIALS

Loew-Cornell Brushes

✻ Series 275 ¾-inch (19mm) oval mop ✻ Series 7000 no. 3 round ✻ Series 7050 no. 1 script liner ✻ Series 7300 nos. 1, 4, 6, 8, 10 and 12 flat shaders ✻ Series 7550 ¾-inch (19mm) and 1-inch (25mm) flat wash ✻ Series 7850 ½ inch (12mm) deer-foot stippler ✻ Series JS no. 1 liner

Additional Supplies

✻ Delta Faux Finish Glaze Base ✻ Krylon Matte Finish Spray ✻ Krylon Acrylic Crystal Clear Protective Clear Coating ✻ gray graphite paper ✻ tracing paper ✻ stylus ✻ chalk pencil

PAINT: DELTA CERAMCOAT ACRYLICS; DECOART AMERICANA (DA)

Dark Burnt Umber	Liberty Blue	Black	Payne's Grey (DA)
Eucalyptus	Gamal Green	White	Moss Green
Burnt Sienna	Butter Yellow	Blue Storm	Butter Cream
Moroccan Red	Black Cherry	Chocolate Cherry	Spice Brown
Fuchsia	Pale Yellow	Quaker Grey	Desert Sun Orange
Golden Brown	Burnt Umber	Bungalow Blue	Sandstone
Charcoal	Medium Foliage Green	Lima Green	Perfect Highlight for Red
Golden Brown + Spice Brown (1:1)			

PATTERNS

These patterns may be hand-traced or photocopied for personal use only. Enlarge at 182 percent to bring up to full size.

PITCHER

1 Clean the enamel tinware surface by washing in the dishwasher, or by hand, with soapy water. Rinse well and let dry completely. Be sure all water is dried from under rolled rims on lid or base of enamel tinware. Spray two thin layers of Krylon Matte Finish Spray onto the tinware surface. Let dry completely between layers of spray. This will give some "tooth" to the surface, enabling acrylic paints to adhere easily. Trace the patterns onto several pieces of tracing paper. It's much easier to transfer a pattern to a curved surface if you separate the pattern into small sections. Using well-worn gray graphite and a stylus, lightly transfer the patterns around the lower edge of the enamel tinware. Use a 1-inch (25mm) flat placed into Faux Finish Glaze Base and then side loaded into a small amount of Dark Burnt Umber. Softly side-load float around all elements on the tinware. Because you are applying a very sheer layer of shading, the Faux Finish Glaze Base allows you to shade without the paint beading up on the surface.

2 Basecoat the pitcher using a 1-inch (25mm) flat with Liberty Blue. It may take up to three layers to establish an opaque basecoat. Let the paint dry completely between basecoat layers. It's much easier to paint over the corner of the cherry scoop and re-establish it later. Using a no. 3 round and Black, basecoat the handle and rim of the pitcher.

3 Before shading, moisten the entire pitcher with clean water. This gives you more "open time" to soften and widen the shading area before the acrylic paint dries. Apply the first layer of shading to the outside edges of the pitcher. Use a 1-inch (25mm) flat, side loaded into Payne's Grey. Let dry completely. Again, moisten. Highlight the center of the pitcher with an oval-shaped highlight of White, softened into the surface while it is still damp. Use a stippling motion, with a dry 3/4-inch (19mm) mop brush. Stipple a background area behind the daisies, using a 1/2-inch (12mm) deerfoot brush and Eucalyptus. .

4 Establish the enamel look by liberally moistening the surface and, while it is still wet, paint thin squiggle lines of White randomly over the surface with a no. 1 script liner. Soften the lines into the surface with a light stipple of a dry 3/4-inch (19mm) mop brush. Using a no. 1 script liner and Gamal Green, paint thin daisy stems to form a daisy bouquet. Paint the main leaves along the stem lines with a no. 8 flat, double loaded into Gamal Green and Eucalyptus. Try to keep a soft moon-shaped bouquet arrangement, which is very pleasing to the eye.

5 Again, dampen the surface. Reinforce the first shaded areas on the pitcher with an additional side-load float of Payne's Grey, using a 1-inch (25mm) flat. Apply the back-to-back highlights on the pitcher handle with a no. 12 flat, side loaded into White. Highlight the rim of the pitcher with a top line of White, painted with a no. 1 liner. Basecoat the petals of the daisy shapes, using the chisel edge of a no. 4 flat generously loaded with Moss Green.

6 Using a 1-inch (25mm) flat, side loaded into Payne's Grey, softly shade under the rim and across the lower edge of the pitcher. Use the chisel edge of a no. 4 flat and a generous amount of White to paint the top daisy petals. Use a no. 1 liner and Gamal Green to paint thin stem lines extending from the bouquet. Let a few stem lines drape over the rim of the pitcher. Use a no. 4 flat with Gamal Green to paint small one-stroke leaves along the stem lines and, as needed, to fill in any holes in the bouquet.

7 Pat the flower centers into the middle of the daisies using a no. 4 flat double loaded into Butter Yellow and Burnt Sienna. Use a 1-inch (25mm) flat placed first into the Faux Finish Glaze Base medium then side loaded into Dark Burnt Umber; float over the bouquet just above the pitcher to "anchor" the floral arrangement into the pitcher. Next, anchor the pitcher to the lower edge of the tinware with a side-load float of Dark Burnt Umber.

8 Use a 1-inch (25mm) flat with Butter Cream to basecoat the jar, until opaque coverage is achieved. Let dry between layers of basecoat. Use a no. 8 flat with Moroccan Red to paint the jar rim and the wide red stripes. Paint the narrower stripes with a no. 4 flat. Two coats may be needed to achieve opaque coverage. To paint the candle glow, dampen the area with clean water and tap on a generous amount of Butter Yellow. Then soften it into the surface with a soft stipple, using a ¾-inch (19mm) dry mop brush.

9 Basecoat the star field area with two coats of Blue Storm on a no. 12 flat. Paint the stars as a thin linework of White, using a no. 1 liner. Shade the blue area under the rim of the jar and down the left side, with a side-load float of Payne's Grey on a no. 12 flat. Paint the candle wick as a line of Dark Burnt Umber. Using a no. 12 flat, side loaded into Black Cherry, shade the top and lower edges of all red stripes, the outside edges of the rim and the inner ellipse of the candle jar rim.

10 Using a no. 12 flat side loaded into Chocolate Cherry, reinforce the red shade areas. Reinforce the blue shade areas with an additional side-load float of Payne's Grey.

11 Use the same brush to shade the Butter Cream areas, under the jar rim and across the bottom of the jar, with a side-load float of Spice Brown. Highlight the front curve of the jar rim with a back-to-back float of Perfect Highlight for Red. Using a no. 1 liner brush and Butter Yellow, paint one comma stroke for the candle flame and highlight it with a small dash of White.

12 Basecoat the flower pot, using a 1-inch (25mm) flat and two coats of Blue Storm. Paint the checkerboard trim across the rim of the flowerpot with a no. 12 flat and thinned White. Shade the outside edges of the flower pot rim, under the rim and around the lower right-hand corner of the flower pot with a 1-inch (25mm) flat, side loaded into Payne's Grey.

13 To paint the geranium leaves, double load a no. 8 flat heavily into Gamal Green and Moss Green. Paint the leaves, following the shapes, with a wiggling motion of the brush. Keep the lighter green to the outside edge of each leaf.

14 Paint some loose vining tendrils and leaf vein lines with thinned Dark Burnt Umber and a no. 1 liner brush.

15 Softly define the geranium areas with a sheer, loose wash of Moroccan Red. Corner load a no. 4 flat heavily into Moroccan Red, and paint tiny "C" strokes randomly to form individual geranium petals over the sheer wash area. Use the same brush and Gamal Green, and sparingly paint small one-stroke leaves along the vining tendrils.

16 Further define the geranium flowers with additional small "C"-shaped petals, using a no. 4 flat that is heavily side loaded into Fuchsia. Casually paint a few Fuchsia individual petals along the vining tendrils to loosen the overall look of the design.

17 Use the same brush and heavily corner load into a mix of Fuchsia, with a touch of White. Paint small "C" strokes, in groups of five, to form a full geranium blossom; then randomly, in groups of three, to form partial geranium blossoms. Paint a few petals to indicate partial blossoms extending out of the arrangement.

18 Dot the centers of the geranium flower blossoms with a no. 1 liner brush tipped into Pale Yellow. Use a no. 12 flat, side loaded sparingly into either Butter Yellow or Black Cherry, and tint the outside edges of some geranium leaves. Deepen the background shading around the Geranium Pot, if needed, with an additional side-load float of Dark Burnt Umber on a 1-inch (25mm) flat.

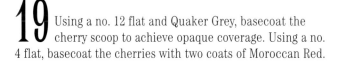

19 Using a no. 12 flat and Quaker Grey, basecoat the cherry scoop to achieve opaque coverage. Using a no. 4 flat, basecoat the cherries with two coats of Moroccan Red.

20 Shade across the bottom of the scoop, both outside edges and along the lower edge of the scoop handle, with a side-load float of Charcoal on a no. 12 flat. Shade one side of each cherry with a side-load float of Chocolate Cherry on a no. 8 flat.

21 Highlight the front of the cherry scoop with a soft side-load float of White on a 1-inch (25mm) flat. Highlight the top edge of the scoop handle with a side-load float of White on a no. 8 flat. Using the same brush, highlight the unshaded side of each cherry with a side-load float of Perfect Highlight for Red.

22 Paint a line of Black, using a no. 1 liner, to form the rim of the cherry scoop. Highlight the center of the rim with a thin line of White. Using the same brush, highlight the bright side of each cherry with a small one-stroke of White, and paint a short stem line into each cherry with a line of Dark Burnt Umber. Anchor the lower edge of the cherry scoop to the tinware with a horizontal side-load float of Dark Burnt Umber on a 1-inch (25mm) flat.

23 Using a no. 3 round and Quaker Grey, basecoat the tin stars.

24 Shade the inner points of the tin stars with top lines of Charcoal, on a no. 3 round. Highlight the outside points of each tin star with top lines of White.

25 Deepen the background shading around the tin stars with a no. 1 flat, placed first in the Faux Finish Glaze Base and then side loaded into Dark Burnt Umber.

26 Accent the tin stars with linework bows of Moroccan Red, painted with a no. 1 liner. Shade the base of the bow loops and "hit-and-miss" on the curves of the bows with top lines of Chocolate Cherry.

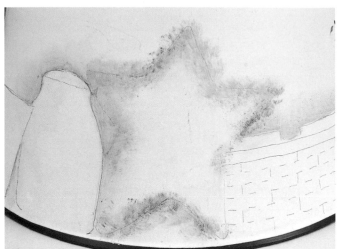

27 Stipple on the background shading, behind the star-shaped berry wreath, with Spice Brown on a ½-inch (12mm) deerfoot stippler.

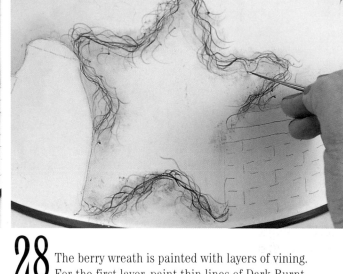

28 The berry wreath is painted with layers of vining. For the first layer, paint thin lines of Dark Burnt Umber, on a no. 1 script liner, loosely around the wreath shape. For the second layer, widen the wreath with an additional layer of thin lines of Burnt Umber.

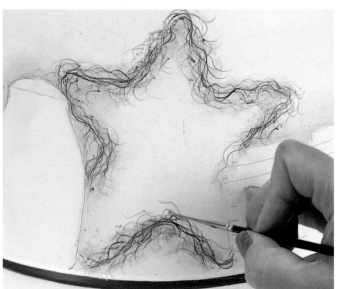

29 Using the same brush, paint a third layer of loose lines using Golden Brown.

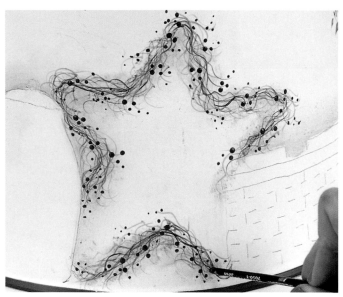

30 Use the handle end of a brush, dipped into Moroccan Red, to paint dot berries randomly around the wreath. Dot several times with the handle end before reloading with more paint and you will achieve a variety of different-sized dot berries.

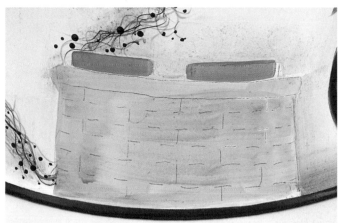

31 Wash the basket with one sheer coat of Golden Brown on a 1-inch (25mm) flat. Paint the clay pot rims with a no. 8 flat and Desert Sun Orange to achieve opaque coverage.

32 Paint the basket spokes, the short vertical lines between the horizontal slats, with a thick line of Golden Brown on a no. 3 round. Paint the horizontal slats on the basket and rim with a no. 8 flat and the appropriate following colors: the red horizontal slats are painted with Moroccan Red, the blue horizontal slats are painted with Blue Storm and the brown horizontal slats are painted with a brush mix of Golden Brown and Spice Brown (1:1). To achieve a "hand-woven" look for your basket, let a thin line of the basecoat color show between the rows of horizontal slats.

33 Shade both ends of the basket rim and the left side of each brown horizontal slat with a side-load float of Spice Brown, on a ³⁄₄-inch (19mm) flat. With the same brush, shade the left side of the red slats with Chocolate Cherry and the left side of the blue slats with Payne's Grey.

34 Add texture to your basket by painting shading lines on the horizontal slats. Use a no. 1 liner and the following shade colors to pull various lengths of lines from the shade area across each slat: use Burnt Umber on the brown slats, Chocolate Cherry on the red slats and Payne's Grey on the blue slats. Shade under the basket rim with a 1-inch (25mm) flat, side loaded into Burnt Umber.

35 Use a no. 10 flat to stroke in the main leaves across the clay pots, with a double load of Gamal Green and Moss Green.

36 Pull loose tendrils from the design area with thinned Gamal Green on a no. 1 liner. With a no. 4 flat loaded into Gamal Green, casually paint small filler leaves along the vining and in the holes in the design.

37 Use a no. 6 flat to stroke in the small flower petals with a double load of Bungalow Blue and White. Keep the Bungalow Blue to the outside of each stroke.

38 Use a no. 4 flat to dab in the flower centers, with a double load of Burnt Sienna and Pale Yellow.

39 With a ³/4-inch (19mm) flat and Sandstone, basecoat the crock till color is opaque. Reapply the pattern lines for the crock lid with a chalk pencil.

40 First, moisten the crock with clean water. Using a 1-inch (25mm) flat, side loaded into Charcoal, softly shade down the left side of the crock. Stipple with a ³/4-inch (19mm) dry mop brush to smooth out the shaded area and remove any brushmarks. Let dry completely. Repeat this procedure as you continue to shade the following areas of the crock: down the right side, the left side of the lid, the knob on the lid and across the bottom of the crock. Use the same moistening technique to apply White highlights to the middle area of the crock, the right edge of the lid and the knob on the lid.

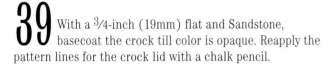

41 With Blue Storm on a no. 1 liner, paint the stem line of the crock strokework design and the rim of the crock lid. Paint the largest comma strokes of the strokework design on the front of the crock, using a no. 3 round and Blue Storm. Use a no. 1 liner and Blue Storm to paint the smaller comma strokes in the strokework design.

42 Reinforce the shade and highlight areas established in Step 40, with an additional side-load float of Payne's Grey for the shade areas and White for the highlight areas. Darken the set-back shading around the crock, if needed, with a 1-inch (25mm) flat placed in Faux Finish Glaze Base then side loaded into Dark Burnt Umber.

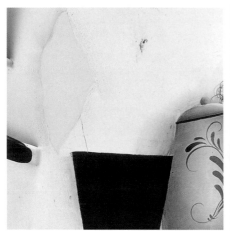

43 Basecoat the pail with two or three layers of Moroccan Red on a 1-inch (25mm) flat. Use the same brush to basecoat the flag with two or three layers of Butter Cream.

44 Reapply pattern lines on the flag and pail. On the pail, use a ¾-inch (19mm) flat, side loaded into Black Cherry to shade below and above the star band and down both sides of the pail. Paint the flag stripes with Moroccan Red on a no. 4 flat. Paint the blue star field with Blue Storm on a no. 8 flat.

45 Basecoat the stars with a no. 4 flat and Charcoal. Use a no. 1 liner and Moroccan Red to paint the ridges above and below the star band. Paint the stars on the blue field of the flag with a no. 1 liner and White. Shade the edges and underneath the fold of the flag with a side-load float of Dark Burnt Umber on a 1-inch (25mm) flat. Paint the flagpole as a line of Burnt Umber, with a no. 1 liner.

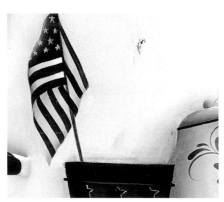

46 Reinforce the shade areas with another side-load float of Chocolate Cherry. Use a no. 1 liner to shade the ridges above and below the star band with a top line of Chocolate Cherry. Highlight the middle of the ridge with a top line mix of Moroccan Red and a touch of White. Line the right side of each star with White. Shade behind the left side of each star with a side-load float of Chocolate Cherry, on a ¾-inch (19mm) flat. Highlight the right side of the two Butter Cream stripes with a side-load float of White on a no. 10 flat; then highlight the left side of the blue star field with a side-load float of White.

47 Paint the stem lines for the fern, from the middle third of the pail, with Gamal Green on a no. 1 script liner.

48 With a no. 4 flat, loaded into Gamal Green, paint the first layer of small one-stroke leaves to form fern fronds along several stem lines. Notice how the leaves become smaller and curve gracefully as they near the tips of the frond.

49 Paint a second layer of fern fronds along some stem lines, with the same brush and Medium Foliage Green. Paint this layer of fronds to fill in between the first layer of fronds and to slightly overlap some areas.

50 Paint the final layer of fern fronds, using the same brush and Medium Foliage Green tipped into Lima Green. Use this color sparingly; just highlight, hit and miss, along the fern fronds. Separate the pail from the red enamel trim, on the lower edge of the camp pot, with a side-load float of Dark Burnt Umber on a 1-inch (25mm) flat. To deepen the set-back shading around the pail and separate it from the crock, use a 1-inch (25mm) flat, placed first into Faux Finish Glaze Base and then side loaded into Dark Burnt Umber.

STROKEWORK BORDER

51 This is Side 1 of the Americana Camp Pot. Accent around the top edge of the camp pot with soft blue "S" strokes of sheer Blue Storm on a no. 6 flat. Let the paint dry completely.

52 Here is Side 2 of the Americana Camp Pot. Spray on a shiny varnish finish with Krylon Acrylic Crystal Clear Protective Clear Coating. Spray several light coats of varnish, and let the camp pot dry completely between layers of varnish.

FIREPLACE SCREEN

A TYPE OF FOLK ART, STARTED IN BALTI-
MORE, MARYLAND, WAS CALLED BALTIMORE SCREEN
PAINTING. IT WAS A WAY TO DECORATE THE FRONT
SCREEN DOORS THAT WERE CLOSE TO THE SIDEWALK.
WHEN WE FOUND THIS FIREPLACE SCREEN, WE REALIZED
THAT THE MESH WAS TIGHT ENOUGH TO ALLOW US TO
PAINT ON IT. USE THIS SCREEN DURING THE SUMMER
WHEN YOU ARE NOT HAVING FIRES IN YOUR FIREPLACE.

MATERIALS

Loew-Cornell Brushes

✶ Series 7550 3/4-inch (19mm) and 1-inch (25mm) flat
wash ✶ Series 7850 1/2-inch (12mm) deerfoot stippler
✶ JS no. 1 liner ✶ Series 7300 nos. 6, 8, 10, 12 and 14
flat shaders ✶ large, stiff household brush

Additional Supplies

✶ large black poster board sheet ✶ white graphite paper
✶ chalk ✶ tracing paper ✶ painter's tape ✶ Rust-Oleum
White Flat Protective Enamel ✶ Krylon Acrylic Crystal
Clear Protective Clear Coating

PAINT: DELTA CERAMCOAT ACRYLICS; DECOART AMERICANA (DA)

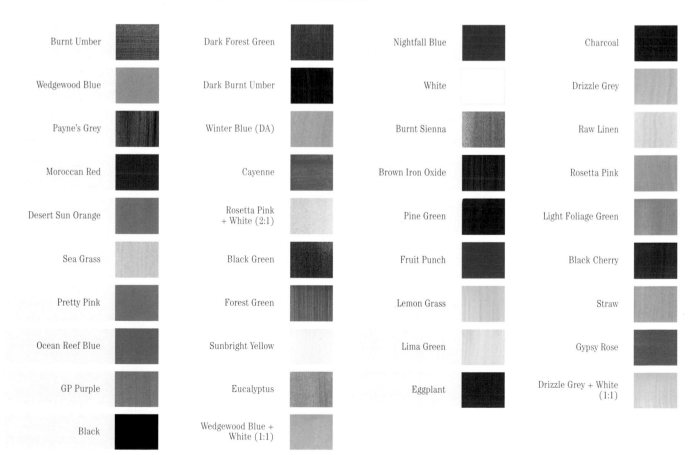

Burnt Umber	Dark Forest Green	Nightfall Blue	Charcoal
Wedgewood Blue	Dark Burnt Umber	White	Drizzle Grey
Payne's Grey	Winter Blue (DA)	Burnt Sienna	Raw Linen
Moroccan Red	Cayenne	Brown Iron Oxide	Rosetta Pink
Desert Sun Orange	Rosetta Pink + White (2:1)	Pine Green	Light Foliage Green
Sea Grass	Black Green	Fruit Punch	Black Cherry
Pretty Pink	Forest Green	Lemon Grass	Straw
Ocean Reef Blue	Sunbright Yellow	Lima Green	Gypsy Rose
GP Purple	Eucalyptus	Eggplant	Drizzle Grey + White (1:1)
Black	Wedgewood Blue + White (1:1)		

PATTERN

This pattern may be hand-traced or photocopied for personal use only. Enlarge at 200 percent, then again at 200 percent, then again at 125 percent to bring up to full size.

Metal Fireplace Screen

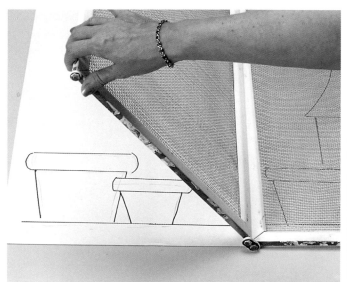

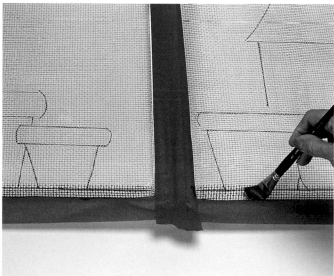

1 Spray the entire screen with Rust-Oleum Flat White Protective Enamel. Allow to dry and cure for a couple of days. Tape off the frame of the screen. Basecoat the screen with Winter Blue, using a large, stiff household brush. Paint both sides of the screen. Transfer the design onto a large black poster board. You may want to enhance the lines with chalk or a white marker so you can see them easier through the screen. Having the poster board behind the screen shows you the design without having to trace it directly on the screen. The poster board also acts as a drop cloth for any paint going through the screen. See step 3, on the next page, to see what happens.

2 Using a 1-inch (25mm) flat, paint the ground with Burnt Umber and Dark Forest Green. Dip your brush alternately into these colors to vary the colors in the ground area.

3 Basecoat the tall birdhouse with Nightfall Blue, using the 1-inch (25mm) flat. The dark blue square that is in the upper right side of the house is blue paint that went through the screen and is on the poster board below. It is not a window, only a blob of paint.

4 Use the same brush, with Charcoal, to shade the left side of the side of the birdhouse, left side of the front, and under the roof.

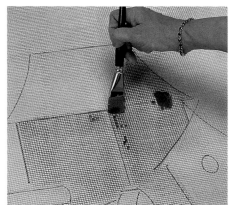

5 Use the same brush and Wedgewood Blue to highlight the right side of the side of the birdhouse, and the right side of the front. You may add some White to the Wedgewood Blue, if needed, to help it show up.

6 Using the same brush, deepen the shadows under the roof with a side-load float of Dark Burnt Umber. With a mix of Wedgewood Blue and White (1:1), stand your brush on the chisel edge and pull some streaks in the wood of the birdhouse.

7 Basecoat the roof and right eave of the roof with Drizzle Grey, using the 1-inch (25mm) flat. Shade the upper left corner of the roof with Payne's Grey, fanning out along the top and left side of the roof. Shade at the top of the eave with Payne's Grey, using the chisel edge of the brush.

8 In the lower right corner, use the same brush to highlight the roof with White. Fan out along the bottom edge and the right side of the roof. Pull some White from the bottom of the eve, using the chisel edge of the brush.

9 Use the same brush, with a side-load float of thinned Burnt Sienna, to randomly apply rust to the edges of the roof.

10 Paint the bird hole with Black, using a no. 12 flat. If needed, you may deepen the shading on the roof with Black, using the 1-inch (25mm) flat.

11 Basecoat the smaller birdhouse, using a no. 12 flat, with Raw Linen. Shade along the left side and under the eaves with a side-load float of Burnt Umber. Highlight the right side with a side-load float of White.

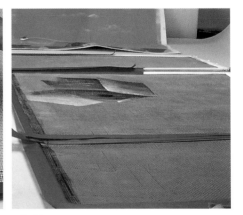

12 If you are having trouble seeing your shading and highlighting, look at the screen from the side. You should be able to see your work.

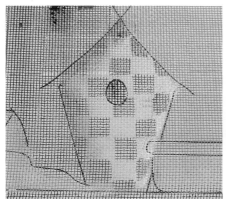

13 Using a 1-inch (25mm) flat, paint checks on the birdhouse with Moroccan Red. Start the checks in the center and at the top, under the peak of the roof. Work your way down and out toward both sides. Allow the checks to dry. Repeat the shading and highlighting of step 11.

14 Using a no. 10 flat, basecoat the twigs with Dark Burnt Umber. Overstroke the twigs with Raw Linen, using a 1-inch (25mm) flat. With the chisel edge of the brush, touch on the top edge and lightly streak over the Dark Burnt Umber, to create a bark effect.

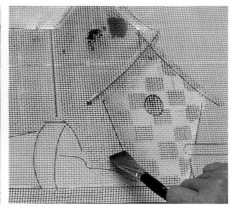

15 Separate the birdhouses with a side-load float of Dark Burnt Umber, using a 1-inch (25mm) flat. This shadow should be on the tall birdhouse, right next to the short birdhouse.

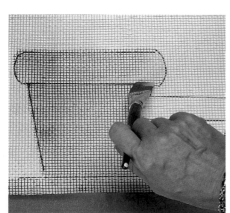

16 Basecoat the four large clay pots with Cayenne, using a 1-inch (25mm) flat. Shade the left sides, along the bottoms and under the rims with a side-load float of Brown Iron Oxide. Highlight the right side of the rims, the lower edge of the rims and middle of the right side of the pots with Rosetta Pink.

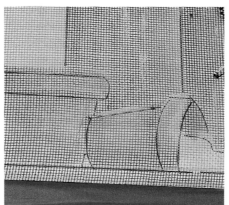

17 Basecoat the four smaller pots with Desert Sun Orange. Shade the left sides, the bottoms and under the rims with Burnt Sienna. Highlight the rims and the right sides with a mix of Rosetta Pink and White (2:1). For the pot on its side, repeat the shading along the ground with Brown Iron Oxide. Highlight the top side of that pot.

18 Use a 1/2-inch (12mm) deer-foot, with touches of Dark Burnt Umber, Dark Forest Green, Raw Linen and Brown Iron Oxide, to stipple in the dirt coming out of the fallen pot.

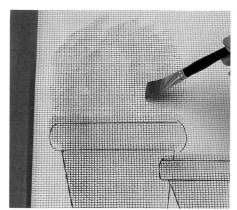

19 Use a 1-inch (25mm) flat, with Dark Forest Green, to lightly paint the background behind the geranium foliage.

20 Use a ¾-inch (19mm) flat and dip the same corner of your brush into Pine Green and Dark Forest Green. Then on the other corner of the brush, dip into Light Foliage Green and Sea Grass. Allow the colors to vary as you paint the leaves. The light color is to the outside of the leaves. Use a no. 1 liner, with Pine Green, to pull some stems to the leaves and blossom areas. Using Burnt Umber, add some fine tendrils coming from the foliage.

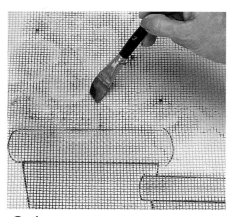

21 Using a ¾-inch (19mm) flat, shade around a few of the front geranium leaves with a side-load float of Black Green. This will separate them from leaves in the background.

22 Roughly set in the areas of the blossoms with Fruit Punch, using a no. 12 flat. Shade the bottom of each area with Black Cherry.

23 Use a no. 6 flat, double loaded with Black Cherry and Pretty Pink, to paint "C"-stroke petals. Occasionally touch the Pretty Pink side into White to brighten and help define the petals.

24 Using a 1-inch (25mm) flat, basecoat the area with Black Green. Use a no. 14 flat, double loaded with Forest Green and Lemon Grass, to stroke on some random leaves.

25 Using a no. 6 flat, paint the daisy petals with strokes of White. Double load the same brush with Burnt Sienna and Straw and paint the centers.

26 Double load a no. 6 flat with Nightfall Blue and Ocean Reef Blue and paint the lobelia with small "C" strokes. Occasionally touch the Ocean Reef Blue corner into White for variation.

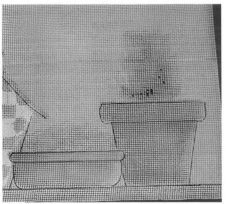

27 Use a 1-inch (25mm) flat and basecoat the background behind the daffodils and herbs with Dark Forest Green.

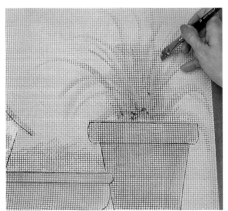

28 Double loaded a no. 14 flat with Lemon Grass and Dark Forest Green and pull long daffodil leaves. Start with your brush flat. As you pull up, turn and lift the brush to the chisel edge. Pull several leaves up and some falling down over the pot. Use the chisel edge, with Dark Forest Green and a touch of Black Green, to pull the stems for the flowers. Shade between the leaves and on the leaves along the top of the pot, with a side-load float of Black Green.

29 Basecoat the flowers with Straw, using a no. 8 flat. Shade the bottom and inside of the trumpet with a "C"-shaped stroke of Burnt Sienna. Highlight the top edges of the trumpet and top edges of the leaves with Sunbright Yellow.

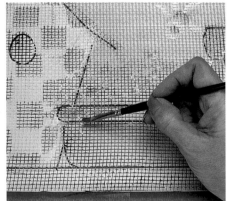

30 Paint one-stroke leaves, using a double load of Pine Green and Lima Green. Allow some leaves to hang over the edge of the pot. Add groups of blossoms with double-loaded "C" strokes of Gypsy Rose and White, using a no. 6 flat. The next group of blossoms are a double load of GP Purple and White, with a center of Sunbright Yellow. The remaining blossoms are a double load of Nightfall Blue and Ocean Reef Blue. Occasionally touch the Ocean Reef Blue side into White for some variation.

31 With a no. 1 liner, and a brush mix (see page 16) of Forest Green and Burnt Umber, to pull some stems of lavender from the pot. Use a no. 12 flat, with Eucalyptus and a touch of Forest Green, to stroke in long leaves along the stems. Then use Pine Green to paint some dark leaves.

32 Make "C" strokes for the lavender blossoms using a no. 6 flat, double loaded with GP Purple and Eggplant. Occasionally, touch the brush into White for some variation in the color of the blossoms.

33 Use a no. 1 liner, with a brush mix of Dark Burnt Umber and Black Green, to add loose vining and branches at each side of the fireplace screen center. Keep the right side shorter than the left side. Using a no. 16 flat, double load Dark Forest Green and Light Foliage Green and stroke some leaves along these vines and branches.

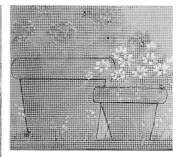

34 Using a 1/2-inch (12mm) deerfoot, stipple the front grass areas with Dark Forest Green and Light Foliage Green. Touch into Lima Green to brighten some areas. Use a no. 1 liner and any of the greens to pull some random grasses. Add some touches of White, Pretty Pink, Ocean Reef Blue and Sunbright Yellow to simulate blossoms among the grasses.

35 Paint the frame of the screen with a mix of Drizzle Grey and White (1:1). Poke out any filled holes in the screen with an open paper clip. It is not necessary to varnish the screen. If you would prefer to for future cleaning purposes, allow the paint to dry thoroughly. Spray with several fine coats of Krylon Acrylic Crystal Clear Protective Clear Coating.

FRUIT AND FLOWER PLATE

China plate

LOOK CLOSELY—THE PAINTED DESIGN IN THE CENTER IS INSPIRED BY THE COLORFUL BORDER OF THIS PLATE. WOULDN'T IT BE FUN TO COLLECT AND PAINT A VARIETY OF BEAUTIFUL DINNER PLATES? WHAT A STUNNING TABLE YOU COULD SET!

MATERIALS

Loew-Cornell Brushes

✶ Series 275 1/2-inch (12mm) oval mop ✶ Series 7050 no. 1 script liner ✶ Series 7300 nos. 6, 8, 10, 14 and 16 flat shaders ✶ Series 7550 3/4-inch (19mm) flat wash ✶ Series 7850 1/4-inch (6mm) deerfoot stippler

Additional Supplies

✶ Krylon Matte Finish Spray ✶ Krylon Acrylic Crystal Clear Protective Clear Coating ✶ gray graphite ✶ stylus ✶ tracing paper

PAINT: DELTA CERAMCOAT ACRYLICS

Leprechaun	Dark Forest Green	Spice Brown	Sachet Pink
Mulberry	Lisa Pink	Royal Plum	Wisteria
Lilac	White	Indiana Rose	Pink Silk
Straw	Burnt Sienna	Medium Foliage Green	Island Coral
Black Cherry	Peachy Keen	Black Green	Stonewedge Green
Bungalow Blue	Island Coral + Black Cherry (1:1)		

PATTERN

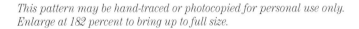

This pattern may be hand-traced or photocopied for personal use only. Enlarge at 182 percent to bring up to full size.

1 Wash the plate thoroughly with warm soapy water. Dry completely. Lightly spray the plate with two layers of Krylon Matte Finish Spray. This will give "tooth" to the surface, and will enable you to paint with regular acrylic paints. Using a light touch, transfer the pattern to the center of the plate with gray graphite and a stylus.

2 Basecoat the main leaves with one sheer layer of Leprechaun.

3 Side load a ³/₄-inch (19mm) flat brush into Dark Forest Green, and shade the base of each leaf. Shade half of each leaf at a time. First shade one side of the leaf. Slide on the chisel edge to form a center vein line. Then shade the other half of the leaf.

4 Load a no. 1 script liner with Spice Brown, and paint the stems and vein lines of the leaves. Also pull a few areas of loose vining from the main design.

5 Basecoat the plums with Sachet Pink on a no. 10 flat. Two coats will be needed to achieve an opaque basecoat.

6 Paint the first layer of shading on the left of the plum closest to the wild rose with a no. 14 flat, side loaded into Mulberry. To achieve a wide side-load float, apply the paint away from the back edge of the object, walk it back and then soften it out.

7 Using a ³/₄-inch flat that is side loaded with Petal Pink, strongly highlight the outside edges of the back petals. Now, strongly highlight the front petals with a side-load float of Hydrangea Pink.

8 Again, using the same brush and color, shade the second plum to separate it from the first.

Thin the paint slightly and stay up on the tip of the brush to paint loose, thin vining lines.

9 Use a no. 14 flat, with an additional side-load float of Mulberry, to deepen the shading in all three areas.

10 Highlight the outside curves of both plums with a soft side-load float of Lisa Pink, on a no. 14 flat.

11 Basecoat all the grapes with Royal Plum, on a no. 8 flat.

12 Double load a no. 8 flat with Royal Plum and Wisteria. Blend very well on your palette. Then repaint the background grapes, highlighting and shading all in one step.

13 Double load a no. 8 flat into Royal Plum and Lilac. Blend very well on your palette, then repaint the foreground grapes. Further highlight a few grapes, to really brighten them, with an additional side-load float of the same brush mix, touched into White on the highlighted half of the brush.

14 Using the same brush, tint a few of the grapes with a sheer wash of Mulberry. This adds a variation of color to the grape cluster. Paint a small highlight dot on each grape with White on a no. 1 script liner.

15 Use a no. 10 flat, and one layer of Indiana Rose, to basecoat the two partial roses in the background.

16 Shade the base of each individual petal with a soft side-load float of Sachet Pink, on a no. 16 flat. Leave a sliver of the basecoat color showing between the petals to maintain the shape of the rose.

17 Load a no. 1 script liner with thinned Mulberry. Pull thin shading lines radiating out from the base of each rose petal.

18 Highlight the outside edges of each rose petal with a strong side-load float of Pink Silk, on a no. 14 flat. Loosen and ruffle the outside edge of the petal by wiggling your brush slightly as you apply the highlight. Let dry completely. Repeat, if needed, to cover your pattern lines or to strengthen the highlight area.

19 Stipple the flower center with Straw, Burnt Sienna and White. Dip a 1/4-inch (6mm) deerfoot stippler into Straw, and dab onto the flower center. Use the same brush, and dip the toe of the brush into Burnt Sienna. Stipple-shade one half of the flower center while it is still wet. Wipe the brush onto dry paper toweling, and tip the toe into White. Stipple a highlight on the opposite side of the flower center.

20 Paint the tiny dots loosely around the outside edge of each flower center, using the tip of a script liner brush and Medium Foliage Green.

21 Basecoat the peach with Island Coral, using a ¾-inch (19mm) flat. You will need two coats to achieve an opaque basecoat.

22 Dampen the peach with a thin wash of clean water to give you more time to apply the shading and make it easier to soften the color. Using a ¾-inch (19mm) flat brush, shade the peach with a side-load float, in a mix of Island Coral and Black Cherry (1:1). Soften the surface by stippling over the shade area with a dry ½-inch (12mm) mop brush. Let dry completely. Deepen the shade areas with an additional side-load float, using the ¾-inch (19mm) flat and a small amount of Black Cherry.

23 Using the same brush, highlight the outside curves of the peach with a side-load float of Peachy Keen.

24 Paint the foreground wild rose, as previously instructed in steps 15 – 20.

25 Tuck the leaves further behind the design elements, or separate one leaf from another, with a sheer side-load float of Black Green on a ¾-inch (19mm) flat.

26 Casually paint shadow leaves along the vining or fill in holes in the design, with thinned Stonewedge Green on a no. 10 flat.

27 Paint the smallest filler leaves with a sheer double load of Stonewedge Green and Bungalow Blue, on a no. 6 flat.

28 Return the plate to a shiny finish, and protect the painted design, with two thin layers of Krylon Acrylic Crystal Clear Protective Clear Coating. This plate is suitable for serving only if you place a clear glass plate over it. To clean the plate, gently hand wash. Do not soak in water or wash in the dishwasher.

ANTIQUE DOUGH BOWL

WHEN WE WERE AT THE FLEA MARKET, WE SAW SEVERAL BOWLS SIM-
ILAR TO THIS. THIS BOWL WAS GIVEN TO US BY JEANNE HENDRICKSON GORIS.
SHE IS THE AUNT OF A GOOD FRIEND, ROSEMARY DEVRIES. IT HAS BEEN WAITING
FOR THE RIGHT PROJECT FOR A LONG TIME. THE
COLORS AND FLORAL DESIGN IN
THIS BOWL WERE INSPIRED
BY THE MATERIAL USED
FOR WINDOW TREATMENTS
AND PILLOWS.

Antique wooden dough bowl

MATERIALS

Loew-Cornell Brushes

✽ Series 7300 nos. 4, 6, 8, 10, 12,
14, 16 and 20 flat shaders
✽ Series 7850 ¹/2-inch (12mm)
deerfoot stippler ✽ JS Liner no. 1
✽ large varnish mop brush

Additional Supplies

✽ stylus ✽ white graphite paper
✽ tracing paper ✽ palette
✽ paper towels; ruler ✽ chalk
pencil ✽ Burnt Umber oil paint
✽ soft cloth ✽ turpentine
✽ J. W. Right-Step Satin Varnish

PAINT: DELTA CERAMCOAT ACRYLICS; DECOART AMERICANA (DA)

Moroccan Red	Sonoma Wine	Raw Linen	English Yew Green
Light Timberline Green	Black Green	Cool Neutral (DA)	Bambi Brown
Dunes Beige + Bambi Brown (2:1)	Dunes Beige	Putty	Dunes Beige + Putty (1:1)
Dusty Purple	Purple Dusk	Black Plum (DA)	Bahama Purple
Wild Rice	Yellow Ochre (DA)	Blue Haze	Gamal Green
Territorial Beige	Tendrils Mix + Raw Linen (3:1)	Red Bkgrd. Mix: Moroccan Red + Sonoma Wine (2:1) + touch of Raw Linen	Tendrils Mix: Red Bkgrd. Mix + Bambi Brown + Cool Neutral (DA) (1:2:2)
English Yew Green + touch of Red Bkgrd. Mix			

PATTERN

This pattern may be hand-traced or photocopied for personal use only. Enlarge at 193 percent to bring up to full size.

LEAVES & TENDRILS

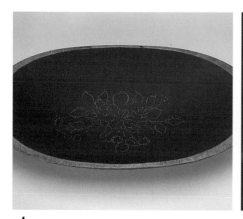

1 Basecoat the inside of the bowl with the Red Background Mix. Allow to dry. Trace the pattern into the center of the bowl.

2 Using a no. 16 flat, basecoat the large leaves with English Yew Green and a touch of the Red Background Mix color.

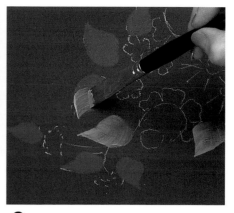

3 Repaint the leaves with the English Yew Green and a touch of Red Background Mix color, working one leaf at a time. While the leaf is still wet, touch the chisel edge of the brush into Light Timberline Green. Starting at the outside edge of the leaf and on the tip of the leaf, touch and streak lightly into the leaves toward the center.

4 Using a no. 20 flat with a side load of Black Green, shade the stem end of the leaf. Then pull down the center of the leaf on the chisel edge of the brush to create the center vein.

5 Using a no. 1 liner with Black Green, add a stem to the leaves and side veins off the center vein. Along some of the leaves, overstroke the outside edge of the leaf with fine lines of Black Green.

6 With the Tendrils Mix color, pull some tendrils out from the background. You will use this mixture later in the project on step 36.

7 Using the same mix of paint with a no. 6 flat, paint one-stroke leaves along these tendrils. Do not overdo this; you may add some later if you need to.

8 With a no. 20 flat and a side-load float of Bambi Brown, paint the four petals at the base of the rose.

9 With the same color and brush, stroke in the back top petals with a fluffy "C" stroke.

10 Create the front petal with a side-loaded "C" stroke, using the same color and brush.

11 Do the same stroke reversed for the other side of the rose.

12 Use a no. 16 flat, with a 2:1 mix of Dunes Beige and Bambi Brown, to highlight the lower four petals with a side-load float.

13 Using a no. 16 flat, paint the second row of petals inside the rose with a side-load float of fluffy "C" strokes, using Dunes Beige.

14 The third row is a smaller side-load float "C" stroke of a mix of Dunes Beige and Putty (1:1).

15 The fourth and final row of petals is a smaller "C" stroke of a side-load float of Putty.

16 The next stroke-layer of color is a fraction of an inch in from the edge of the petals, using the no. 16 flat with a side-load float of Dunes Beige.

17 The layer of color just inside of the previous stroke is a side-load float of the mix of Dunes Beige and Putty (1:1).

18 Add the final layer of color just inside of the last stroke, with a side-load float of Putty on a no. 14 flat.

19 Using the three levels of colors as in steps 16 – 18, add more "S" strokes to the front of the rose, using a no. 14 flat.

20 With a no. 12 flat, shade the base of the rose and inside of the bowl with a side-load float of the original basecoat color (Red Background Mix).

21 Using a no. 10 flat, with a side-load float of the Dunes Beige and Putty mix (1:1), pull in some small petals at the base of the rose.

22 With a no. 1 liner, add dots of Putty in the center of each rose.

23 Double load a no. 20 flat with Purple Dusk and Dusty Purple. Three-fourths of the brush should be Dusty Purple and one-fourth should be Purple Dusk. Blend slightly on your palette. With the Purple Dusk side to the outside of the petals, stand the brush on the chisel edge, wiggle the brush back and forth slightly to create the width of the petal and return to the chisel edge for the other side of the petal.

24 Using a no. 8 flat, roughly tap in the centers with Black Plum.

25 Use the same brush, still loaded with Black Plum, and touch one corner into Bahama Purple. Tap around the outside of the center, keeping the Bahama Purple to the outer edge of the center.

26 With a side-load float of Bahama Purple, use a no. 16 flat to highlight any petal that lays over another petal. This will help to separate the upper and lower flowers.

27 Using the same colors as the mum petals, paint three or four petals close to each other to make a mum bud.

28 Using a no. 8 flat with English Yew Green, paint two one-stroke leaves at the base of the mum buds to make a calyx.

29 Using a no. 10 flat, double loaded with the Red Background Mix and Wild Rice, add four or five petal stroke flowers. See technique on page 14.

30 Using the same brush with the same colors, add some fall-away blossoms trailing off from the main flowers. This is the same stroke flower, only smaller.

31 Using a no. 6 flat, roughly tap in the centers with Yellow Ochre.

32 Using the same brush loaded with Yellow Ochre, tap one corner of the brush into Sonoma Wine, and shade the side of the center closest to the center of the bowl.

33 With a side-load float of Blue Haze, use a no. 6 flat to add a "C" stroke on the other side of the center.

34 Using a stylus or a no. 1 liner, add dots of Yellow Ochre around the shade side of the center.

35 Use a no. 1 liner and load the brush with Gamal Green, then tip into Blue Haze. Pull one long main stem with several short lines fanning off from the top of the stem.

36 Using a 1/2-inch (12mm) deerfoot, lightly stipple the background flowers with the Tendrils Mix. You may add a touch of Raw Linen to brighten it.

37 Using the wood end of a small brush, dot on top of the stippled area with Yellow Ochre.

109

38 Double load a no. 6 flat with Dunes Beige and Territorial Beige. Paint a small cluster of four-petal flowers trailing off into fall-away blossoms.

39 Using the wood end of a small brush or a stylus, dot the centers with Yellow Ochre.

40 Using a no. 4 flat, basecoat the berries with Dusty Purple. Shade the stem end of the berries with a side-load float of Black Plum.

41 Using the same brush, highlight the berries with a side-load float of Purple Dusk. Repeat the highlight on some of the berries with Bahama Purple. Look over your painting and see if you need to fill in any spaces with additional leaves or filler flowers.

42 Measure one inch down from the top edge and draw a line around the bowl with a chalk pencil. Using a no. 1 liner, paint the fine-line scrolls with the Tendrils Mix paint mixture.

43 Using a no. 8 flat with the same mixture, add some one-stroke leaves along the scroll lines. Allow the painting to dry thoroughly. Erase any visible tracing lines. Using a very large mop brush, varnish the bowl with one coat of satin varnish. We recommend using a large mop brush for varnishing, since it does not leave ridges like the sides of a flat brush does. Allow the varnish to dry thoroughly.

44 To antique the bowl, use a soft cloth dampened with turpentine, then touch into Burnt Umber oil paint. (Winsor & Newton or Alexander's has a nice red undertone to their Burnt Umber oil paint). Rub along the top edge of the bowl, allowing the color to come down slightly onto the Red Background Mix color. This makes a nicer transition for the old wood-stained edge of the bowl and the painted surface. Allow the antiquing to dry twenty-four hours before finishing with two to three more coats of satin varnish.

EDGE BORDER

SNOWMAN CHAIR

Old wooden folding chair

WE LOVE FOLDING CHAIRS, AND THIS SNOWMAN DESIGN LOOKS SO CUTE ON THIS ANTIQUE CHAIR! WOULDN'T IT BE FUN TO MAKE THIS CHAIR THE SPECIAL SEAT FOR YOUR CHILD OR GRANDCHILD AT THE HOLIDAY TABLE! OR YOU COULD JUST TUCK IT IN THE CORNER OF YOUR FAMILY ROOM AND NESTLE A FEW OF YOUR FAVORITE CLOTH SNOWMEN ON ITS SEAT.

MATERIALS

Loew-Cornell Brushes

✳ Series 410 1/4-inch (6mm) and 1/2-inch (12mm) deerfoot stipplers ✳ Series 7050 no. 2 script liner ✳ Series 7300 nos. 2, 4, 10, 14 and 16 flat shaders ✳ Series 7550 1-inch (25mm) flat wash ✳ JS no. 1 liner

Additional Supplies

✳ sandpaper and/or hand-held sander ✳ tracing paper ✳ white graphite paper ✳ J. W. Right-Step Satin Varnish ✳ stylus ✳ paper towels

PAINT: DELTA CERAMCOAT ACRYLICS; DECOART AMERICANA (DA)

Blue Storm	Payne's Grey	Purple Smoke	Black Green (DA)
Dark Forest Green	Spice Brown	Desert Sand (DA)	Medium Foliage Green
Bungalow Blue	Bridgeport Grey	Drizzle Grey	White
Charcoal	Black	Golden Brown	Butter Yellow
Mistletoe (DA)	Opaque Red	Chocolate Cherry	Perfect Highlight for Red
Tangerine	Tangerine (DA)	Burnt Umber	Burnt Sienna
Dark Burnt Umber			

PATTERN

Strokework pattern for step 35

These patterns may be hand-traced or photocopied for personal use only. Enlarge at 200 percent to bring up to full size.

BACKGROUND & TREES

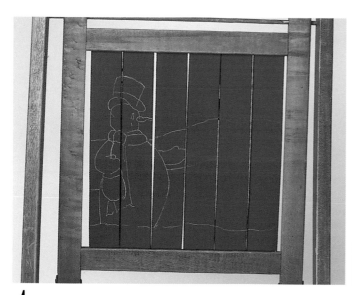

1 Sand the areas where the chair will be painted in order to remove varnish and smooth the wood. Basecoat the seat and back of the chair with two layers of Blue Storm. Use white graphite paper and tracing paper to transfer the pattern onto the chair back.

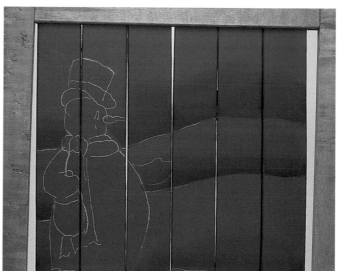

2 Use the 1-inch (25mm) flat, side loaded into Payne's Grey, to paint the background shading behind the hill areas. Moisten behind the hills with a thin layer of water before applying the shading, in order to achieve a soft look. Then the shading will blend softly into the background.

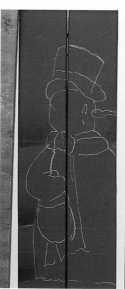

3 Add the background trees. Dampen the surface with clean water, using the 1-inch (25mm) flat. Use the no. 1 liner to lightly sketch in the branches. While the surface is still damp, stipple the tops of the trees onto the surface, using a 1/2-inch (12mm) deerfoot tipped into Purple Smoke. Let the paint bleed into the background to create a soft background scene.

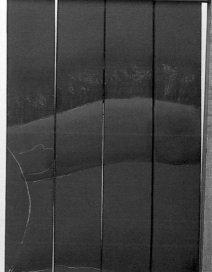

4 Wet the back hill with clean water. Highlight the top of the back hill with a wide side-load float of Purple Smoke, side loaded on a 1-inch (25mm) flat.

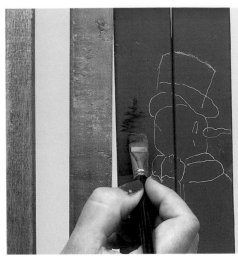

5 With Black Green and Dark Forest Green double loaded on a no. 16 flat, stipple in the background trees. Start on the chisel edge of the brush to paint the top point of the tree. Then stipple with the brush horizontally, as you tap in the branches.

6 Use the no. 2 script liner, loaded into slightly thinned Spice Brown and then pulled through a little Desert Sand, to paint the bare trees onto the design. Hold the brush back on the handle. Roll it back and forth gently while you paint the branches to achieve loose, natural-looking branches.

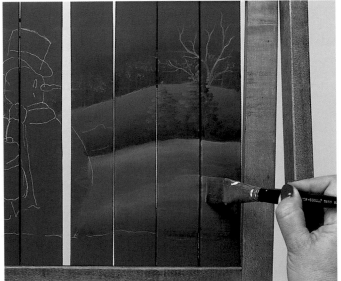

7 Double load the no. 16 flat with Black Green and Dark Forest Green. Then tip the Dark Forest Green side into a little Medium Foliage Green, and stipple the pine trees onto the design. As you work from the back to the front of this design, the center pine trees should be a little brighter than the background pine trees.

8 When the pine trees are completely dry, set them into the hillside with a side-load float of Payne's Grey on a 1-inch (25mm) flat over the bottom of the trees. Using the same brush, side loaded into Purple Smoke and a touch of Bungalow Blue and working on a moistened surface, highlight the hill in front of the center pine trees.

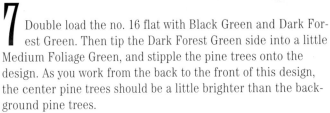

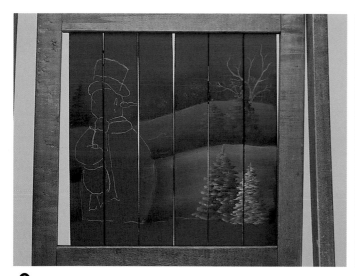

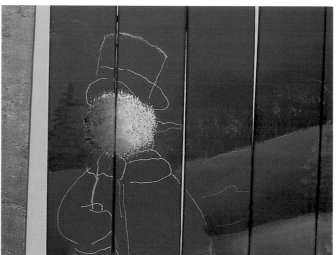

9 Shade behind the tummy of the snowman with a side-load float of Payne's Grey on a no. 16 flat. Add the front trees with a no. 16 flat double loaded into Black Green and Medium Foliage Green, then tipped into a little White on the Medium Foliage Green side of the brush. Stipple in these trees as you did the previous pine trees.

10 Stipple basecoat the snowman's head with the ½-inch (12mm) deerfoot and Bridgeport Grey. While the basecoat is still wet, wipe the brush on paper toweling to remove some paint. Then put the toe of the brush into Payne's Grey and blend well on the palette. Do not wash out the brush between steps. Stipple shade on the left side of the snowman's head with Payne's Grey.

11 Wipe the ½-inch (12mm) deerfoot well on dry paper toweling before loading with the next color. Highlight the right side of the head with a stipple of Drizzle Grey. Wipe the brush and highlight further with White.

12 Repeat the same stippling steps on the body and partial arm of the snowman. The arm holding the basket will be painted after the scarf is completed.

13 With a no. 10 flat, basecoat the hat with Charcoal and the hat band with Golden Brown. Using the same brush, shade the hat with a side-load float of Black. Highlight the hat with a side-load float of Drizzle Grey double loaded onto the brush with Charcoal. Shade the hatband with a side-load float of Golden Brown touched into a small amount of Chocolate Cherry. Highlight the opposite side of the hatband with a side-load float of Butter Yellow.

14 Use a no. 1 liner and Mistletoe to add the trim lines. The stripe along the top edge of the hatband is painted as a line of Opaque Red. Edge the hat brim with a fine line of White.

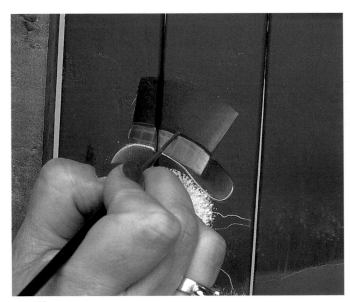

15 Use the no. 10 flat to reinforce the shading on the hatband with an additional side-load float of Chocolate Cherry. Highlight the front edge with an additional side-load float of Butter Yellow touched into a little White. Highlight the front edge of the Opaque Red trim line with a top line of Perfect Highlight for Red.

16 Realign the pattern and transfer the face and pipe onto the snowman. Using a no. 2 flat, basecoat the eyes with Black, the nose with Tangerine (Delta) and the pipe with Golden Brown. Use the corner of the brush to paint little smudges of coal for his mouth with Black. Using a no. 10 flat and Opaque Red, basecoat the scarf till the color is opaque.

17 Wet the cheek area with clean water, and add blush with a soft tap of Opaque Red on the corner of a no. 10 flat. Detail the eye with a side-load float of Purple Smoke on a no. 2 flat. Add the sparkle to the eye with a small dot of White on the tip of a no. 1 liner. Use the no. 10 flat, side loaded into Chocolate Cherry, to shade the nose where it tucks into the face and along the lower edge of the nose.

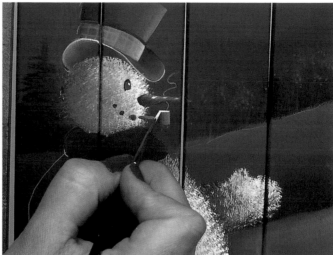

18 Highlight the snowman's nose with a side-load float of Tangerine (DecoArt) along the top edge, painted with a no. 10 flat. Further highlight with small dashes of White, painted with the chisel edge of the no. 10 flat.

19 Use the same brush to shade the pipe, where it goes into the snowman's mouth, and down the left side of the pipe bowl with a side-load float of Chocolate Cherry. Add a thin curling line of smoke coming out of the pipe with Bridgeport Grey on a no. 1 liner. Highlight the top edge of the pipe bowl with a tiny highlight dash of White on a no. 1 liner. To set the features into the face, shade to the left of each feature with a soft side-load float of Charcoal on a no. 10 flat. Hold the brush at approximately a 30° angle while shading behind each element.

20 Soften the line between the head and hat with a soft stipple of Bridgeport Grey on the toe of a 1/2-inch (12mm) deerfoot.

21 Using a no. 10 flat, shade the scarf with a side-load float of Chocolate Cherry and highlight with a side-load float of Perfect Highlight for Red.

22 Paint the stripes on the scarf with a no. 1 liner and Mistletoe. Reinforce the shade and highlight areas as instructed in step 21.

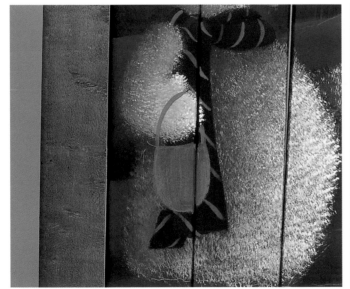

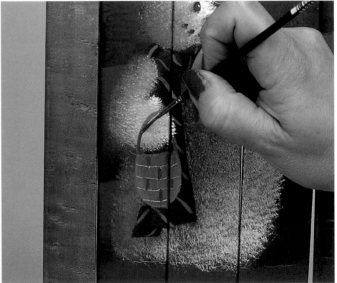

23 Stipple in the front arm and hand, using the same colors, brush and method as instructed for the head and body (see steps 10 – 12.) When you are painting the thumb of the hand, drop down to the 1/4-inch (6mm) deerfoot. Basecoat the basket with Golden Brown, using a no. 10 flat for the basket and a no. 1 liner for the basket handle.

24 Reapply the basket pattern lines. Paint the short vertical lines of the basket with a no. 1 liner and Spice Brown. Shade the area where the handle goes into the basket with a top line of Spice Brown.

25 Use a no. 4 flat, double loaded into Golden Brown and Spice Brown, to weave the basket by painting horizontal stripes between each vertical line. Keep the Golden Brown side of the brush towards the top of the basket.

26 Add some detail line work to the basket with a double load of Burnt Umber and Golden Brown, on a no. 1 liner. Paint the braiding around the basket handle, and add thin shading lines on each horizontal basket slat.

27 Shade the left side of the basket with a side-load float of Burnt Sienna, on a no. 16 flat. Highlight the opposite side of the basket with a side-load float of Golden Brown, touched into a little White. Use the chisel edge of the no. 16 flat to add a highlight dash on the basket handle.

28
Highlight the top of the foreground hill using a 1-inch (25mm) flat, double loaded into Purple Smoke and Bungalow Blue, with a little White added to the Bungalow Blue side of the brush. Add a little more White onto the brush as you streak in the snowdrifts.

29
Paint the bare branches of the foreground bushes with a no. 1 liner and Dark Burnt Umber. Anchor the bushes into the scene, with a side-load float of White on a no. 10 flat, across the bottom of each bush. Dot berries onto the bushes with the handle end of a brush and Opaque Red.

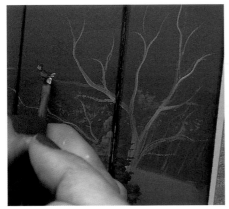

30
Basecoat the birds with a no. 2 flat and Opaque Red. Highlight the front of the face and the tummy with a side-load float of Tangerine (DecoArt). Slide the chisel edge of the no. 2 flat, double loaded into Opaque Red and Tangerine, to form the tail feathers of the bird.

31
Paint the bird beak as very small one-strokes of Black, and dot the eye with Black, using a no. 1 liner. Using the tip of the liner brush, paint dots of birdseed in the snowman's hand. Scatter some birdseed over the snow, at the base of the snowman, with the following colors: Golden Brown, Butter Yellow and Burnt Sienna.

32
Paint snowflakes on the seat of the chair, using a no. 1 liner and Drizzle Grey. Paint a variety of shapes and sizes, in a random pattern, for the most pleasing appearance.

33 Add fun details to the chair frame. Paint checks on the side bars of the chair with Opaque Red, on a no. 14 flat.

34 On the seat corners, use Burnt Umber on a no. 1 liner, to paint branches. Paint the dot berries with the tip of the liner brush and Opaque Red. Using the same brush, paint the ribbon with a thin linework of Blue Storm.

35 Basecoat the top cross rail of the chair with two layers of Blue Storm, using a 1-inch (25mm) flat. Use a no. 10 flat, filled with Purple Smoke, to paint the strokework pattern across the cross rail. Paint small dashes at the base of each stroke sequence with a no. 1 liner and Purple Smoke.

36 Brush on two or three layers of J. W. Right-Step Satin Varnish. Let cure twenty-four hours and sand lightly between layers of varnish.

PROJECT 11: LADYBUG TRIKE BIKE

PAINT

Delta Ceramcoat Acrylics

☆ Bright Red
☆ Black Cherry
☆ Black ☆ Orange
☆ Perfect Highlight
for Red ☆ White
☆ Ocean Reef Blue
☆ Midnight Blue
☆ Rouge

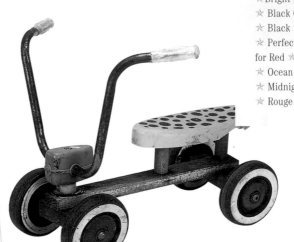

Child's Trike Bike

1 Spray the bike with flat red paint. When dry, rebasecoat with Bright Red. The handle bars and wheels are Black. Shade the seat with Black Cherry and highlight with Orange. The dots are Black, highlighted with a soft grey mix and shaded behind with Black Cherry.

2 The eyes are Ocean Reef Blue with a pupil of Midnight Blue. Highlight with dots of White. The cheeks are a side-load float of Rouge, strengthened with Perfect Highlight for Red and a White line for shine. The mouth lines and hair tendrils are a soft grey mix.

3 The wheel's whitewalls are White, with checks of Bright Red, using a no. 12 flat. The center rivet is Black.

If you plan to use your Ladybug Bike outdoors, use 5 to 6 coats of exterior-grade varnish and let dry completely.

PROJECT 12: GLASS VASE WITH BERRIES

Plain glass vase

PAINT

Delta PermEnamels for
Tile, Glass & Ceramics

Fuchsia ✶ Bordeaux
✶ Pillow Pink ✶ Pine
Green ✶ Marshmallow
✶ Mediterranean Blue
✶ Citrus Yellow ✶
Red Red ✶ Limeade
✶ Celestial ✶ Wisteria

Be sure to follow the
directions on the paint
bottle label when paint-
ing on glass or other
reflective surface.

1 Cut a small sponge into strawberry shapes. Damp-en them, then dip them into Fuchsia. Blend the paint into the surface by tapping in onto your palette. Load one corner into Bordeaux and the other corner into Pillow Pink. Tap gently on your palette to blend colors.

2 Stamp the loaded sponge onto the glass vase to make strawberry shapes in several places. Cut some leaf shapes from the damp sponge. Dip them into Pine Green, then tip half into Mediter-ranean Blue. Stamp them over the berry shape. With a liner, add the hull leaves and a stem.

3 For grapes, cut small round shapes from the sponge and dip into Celestial, then tip into Bordeaux. Overlap some circles. Add leaves and stems just like you did on the strawberries. If you want, add cherries using Red Red; side load one corner into Bordeaux. For foreground cherries, dip one corner into Pillow Pink.

4 Here's the finished vase, ready for summer enter-taining. Be sure to let all the paint dry and cure thorough-ly. And hand-wash your paint-ed glassware rather than put it in the dishwasher—it will last longer and keep its bright colors.

RESOURCES

PAINTS

Delta Ceramcoat Acrylics
Delta PermEnamels for
Tile, Glass & Ceramics

Delta Technical Coatings, Inc.
2550 Pellissier Place
Whittier, CA 90601
Phone: (800) 423-4135
Fax: (562) 695-5157
Web site: www.deltacrafts.com

DecoArt Americana Acrylics

DecoArt
P.O. Box 327
Stanford, KY 40484
Phone: (606) 365-3193
Fax: (606) 365-9739
E-mail: paint@decoart.com
Web site: www.decoart.com

BRUSHES

Loew-Cornell
563 Chestnut Ave.
Teaneck, NJ 07666
Phone: (201) 836-7070
Fax: (201) 836-8110
Web site: www.loew-cornell.com

CANADIAN RETAILERS

Crafts Canada
2745 29th St. N.E.
Calgary, AL, T1Y 7B5

Folk Art Enterprises
P.O. Box 1088
Ridgetown, ON, N0P 2C0
Tel: 888-214-0062

MacPherson Craft Wholesale
83 Quenn St. E.
P.O. Box 1870
St. Mary's, ON, N4X 1C2
Tel: 519-284-1741

Maureen McNaughton Enterprises, Inc.
RR #2
Belwood, ON, N0B 1J0
Tel: 519-843-5648
Fax: 519-843-6022
E-mail: maureen.mcnaughton.ent.inc@
sympatico.ca
Web site:
www.maureen.mcnaughton.com

Mercury Art & Craft Supershop
332 Wellington St.
London, ON, N6C 4P7
Tel: 519-434-1636

Town & Country Folk Art Supplies
93 Green Lane
Thornhill, ON, L3T 6K6
Tel: 905-882-0199

U.K. RETAILERS

Art Express
Index House
70 Burley Road
Leeds LS3 1JX
0800 731 4185
www.artexpress.co.uk

Atlantis Art Materials
146 Brick Lane
London E1 6RU
020 7377 8855

Crafts World (head office)
No. 8 North Street
Guildford
Surrey GU1 4 AF
07000 757070

Green & Stone
259 King's Road
London SW3 5EL
020 7352 0837

Hobby Crafts (head office)
River Court
Southern Sector
Bournemouth International Airport
Christchurch
Dorset BH23 6SE
0800 272387

Homecrafts Direct
PO Box 38
Leicester LE1 9BU
0116 251 3139

INDEX

THE BEST IN DECORATIVE PAINTING INSTRUCTION IS FROM NORTH LIGHT BOOKS!

The Complete Book of Decorative Painting

This book is the must-have one-stop reference for decorative painters, crafters, home decorators and do-it-yourselfers. It's packed with solutions to every painting challenge, including surface preparation, lettering, borders, faux finishes, strokework techniques and more! You'll also find five fun-to-paint projects designed to instruct, challenge and entertain you—no matter what your skill level.

ISBN 1-58180-062-2, paperback, 256 pages, #31803-K

Beautiful Brushstrokes Step by Step

With Maureen McNaughton as your coach, you can learn to paint an amazing array of fabulous leaves and flowers with skill and precision. She provides start-to-finish instruction with hundreds of detailed photos. Beautiful Brushstrokes is packed with a variety of techniques, from the most basic to more challenging strokes, as well as 5 gorgeous strokework projects.

ISBN 1-58180-381-8, paperback, 128 pages, #32396-K

Pretty Painted Furniture

Add beauty and elegance to every room in your home! Diane Treirweiler shows you how with step-by-step instructions for giving old furniture a facelift and new furniture a personal touch. Twelve lovely projects, complete with helpful color charts and traceable patterns, teach you how to paint everything from berries to butterflies on chests, chairs, tables and more.

ISBN 1-58180-234-X, paperback, 128 pages, #32009-K

Painting Gilded Florals and Fruits

Learn how to enhance your paintings with the classic elegance of decorative gold, silver and variegated accents. Rebecca Baer illustrates detailed gilding techniques with step-by-step photos and invaluable problem-solving advice. Perfect for your home or gift giving, there are 13 exciting projects in all, each one enhanced with lustrous leafing effects.

ISBN 1-58180-261-7, paperback, 144 pages, #32126-K

These books and other fine North Light titles are available from your local art & craft retailer, bookstore, online supplier or by calling 1-800-448-0915.